THE LAITY TODAY AND TOMORROW

THE LAITY
TODAY AND TOMORROW

Edmund Flood,O.S.B

PAULIST PRESS
New York/Mahwah

Library of Congress Cataloging-in-Publication Data

Flood, Edmund.
    The laity today and tomorrow.

    Bibliography: p.
    1. Laity—Catholic Church.   2. Catholic Church—Government.
3. Catholic Church—Doctrines.   I. Title.
BX1920.F63   1986   262'.15   86-25413
ISBN 0-8091-2848-9 (pbk.)

Published by Paulist Press
997 Macarthur Boulevard
Mahwah, New Jersey 07430

Printed and bound in the
United States of America

Contents

PART 1
THE QUESTION

The Church is changing. Is that good or bad?

The most obvious changes are in *what people do*. Lay people are giving Communion, reading at Mass, and sometimes even preaching.

But the deeper change is in *what every Catholic is being asked to do*. He or she is being asked to be a partner, not a "hand," in the Church's work. "You have gifts. You are needed as a responsible, mature Christian. And your own Christian life will be incomplete if you do not share, in your own way, in the work of Christ for the world."

We find ourselves having to cope with a situation that's entirely different to what many of us used to know.

How do you and the people you know feel about this? Are you one of the people who feel that we're losing the stability, the peace—even the sense of the sacred—that we need from religion? Or are you one of the people who have experienced the new ways and found them enriching?

The speed of change, in so many of the Church's ways, has left many of us a bit breathless. Quite a number feel confused and even resentful. As brothers and sisters in Christ's family, we want to overcome our differences and go where the Spirit leads us. Unless we do this together, will we really be Christ's body?

We know the only way we can make that possible. Each of us has to place ourself in the presence of God: to forget our selfishness and let ourself be inspired and guided by God's Spirit who is in us.

That will give us an openness to God's ways, in the Church and in the world.

First we shall want to explore God's fullest self-expression so far: the life we see in the New Testament. This will give us a yardstick we can all share to measure what is happening today.

Yes, these *are* difficult times for many of us. We'd have to be very blind or self-centered not to see that. But if we manage to take this little journey together in the presence of God, this book cannot be a gloomy one. God's kingdom *will* come. We are the "good news" people.

You, me, all the Christians we see: to each of us has been given some part of the creative power of God. One reason why Scripture will start us well on our journey is that it will remind us of that "good news" in each other. Increasingly it will open our eyes and hearts to the people—all God's people—whom we are called to travel with.

At first sight, these people—like Jesus himself—may not look like much. But, from Abraham to Paul, doesn't the Bible show so many people being surprised by the discovery of the God who has come to live in the very ordinary people we know? (Jn 1:14).

The only reason that Christianity ever started was that they *had* to tell of that joy. We have a story to tell

I hope that this book will help some people reflect on what is happening in our Church—particularly our parish—today, and what is likely to happen tomorrow. And I hope that our reflection will help us to become more conscious of God's creative presence in our world and of the joy which that brings to all those who respond to his call.

In Part 2 we shall try to open ourselves to the fuller and deeper kind of Christian life which the Bible is there to hold out to us. The experience of God that people had in the New Testament will give us the surest yardstick of all by which to measure the present and the future.

Then, in Part 3, we shall look at three fundamental movements in the Church today and consider what these are already giving to millions of Catholics.

Finally, in Part 4, we shall consider a wider range of contemporary movements and options, and try to assess which direction they are inviting us all to go in the future.

PART 2
NOW AND THEN

Chapter 1
Jesus

In 1981, the parish priest of Elk Grove Village, Illinois reminded his parishioners: "Our business is the reign of God; and our strategy, the only way we will achieve it, is the inner spiritual conversion of all men and women to God in Christ Jesus."[1]

He told them that of course he couldn't accomplish this alone. So he asked them to join him in a strategy by which every person in the area, at the end of five years, would have been given the chance to hear the call of Christ.

That priest wanted God to "reign" in Elk Grove Village. He wanted God's powerful, gracious love to touch and transform the lives of all his neighbors. By using that word "reign" he was reminding himself and his parishioners of those extraordinary two or three years in Palestine when the beginnings of that reign were seen.

"THY KINGDOM COME"

What kind of reign or kingdom did Jesus bring? If we can answer that question, we know what we are praying for when we say the *Our Father*. When we pray "thy kingdom come" is it only a prayer for a life after death?

Perhaps the best way to answer that vital question is for each of us to let all the evidence from the Gospels we can remember flood into our consciousness. That sick person; that disgusting, demented person; that despised and rejected person: each noticed that Jesus cared. He didn't offer only his compassion or only his practical help, but above all his friendship.

Jesus' invitation to us then and now is to set his treatment of the sick, the deranged, the tax-collectors—anyone who needed him—alongside his stories. These stories, or parables, were *the clues he gave to help his audiences understand what was going on in front of them:* how the "kingdom" or "reign" of God is starting to happen in our midst.

SOME PARABLES

Each of us will think of different parables. It may be the warmth, celebration and forgiveness in the *Prodigal Son*; the practical help arising from deep compassion in the *Good Samaritan*; the sense of joyful recovery in the *Lost Sheep*. Each of those stories was told to help people recognize that God was in that ordinary man Jesus, whom they could touch and see and hear, reaching out to people with love and compassion and transforming the lives of all who chose to respond to him.

THE NAZARETH MANIFESTO

Some of us may prefer to start with Jesus' first announcement of God's kingdom. His audience that afternoon, in the synagogue in Nazareth, had always been sure that God's kingdom would one day come. That God himself would come to rule his people had long been promised.

Would Jesus this afternoon say something about that? What

text would he choose? Would it help to explain why he was so different: why he wouldn't join the resistance movement to push the Romans out of their country? Why had he recently gone down to Jordan and joined John, a kind of prophet? When he had read his chosen text, would he simply go back to his place or sit down to show that he wanted to use his right to comment?

The text Jesus chose described what he believed would happen through him. It was his public manifesto of the kingdom:

> The Spirit of the Lord is upon me,
> because he has chosen me to bring good news to the poor.
> He has sent me to proclaim liberty to the captives
> and recovery of sight to the blind;
> to set free the oppressed
> and announce that the time has come
> when the Lord will save his people (Lk 4:18-19).

His business wasn't with words or vague promises for the future. It was to change the situation of actual people. From prison, freedom; from blindness, the amazing joy of sight.

OUR PRAYER TODAY

All that, we may sometimes think, was far away and long ago. But when Jesus followed the custom of his time by summing up for his closest friends his teaching in a prayer, he taught them to say the *Our Father*. He wants us to have as our dearest wish "Thy will be done, thy kingdom come," and to count on this as the supreme gift from "Our Father." He wants me to really care that the people around me have a chance of experiencing that at the center of all life is that reaching out of God in love; that we can really call God our Father who loves and supports us; that we are all really brothers and sisters; and that his "will" is the most marvelous thing for each of us that could be.

He wants us to know, therefore, that not pointlessness but hope has the final word in human life.

NEW HORIZONS

Today we are rediscovering the excitement of that.

Many things are helping us to rediscover the fact that there is a God in the world.

There is a promise of a springtime. But it is a troubled, sometimes stormy spring.

It isn't only the relevance and the attractiveness of God's rule among us that has come into view. If that had been all, most of us could have relaxed and let bishops and priests get on with it. The problem is the voices we hear saying that bringing the news of God's reaching out to all is the job of *all* Christians.

Many Catholics are not comfortable with that. Have most lay people got either the time or competence to talk about their faith to others? Isn't that, anyway, the job of the clergy?

Then other questions arise. The priests are so busy managing the parishes that perhaps they have little opportunity of announcing the good news? And what is the job of a lay Christian? Just to pray, pay and avoid sin? Are his or her talents, education, and experience of the "world" of no account in the drama of the world's greatest opportunity?

By turning to the New Testament accounts of how the Christian communities then lived, we may see what are our respective roles and learn much more about the task that calls us.

Chapter 2
Paul

Paul's letters offer us the fullest and earliest picture in the New Testament of how ordinary people believed they should live as Christians.

But aren't there great blemishes in that picture? What kind of guide to Christian life today is a man who thought of women as inferior?

The irony is that Paul profoundly believed that women should be equal to men in the Church, and he had persuaded even the reactionaries in his communities to take that equality for granted. Later on we'll come to the evidence about this. But first let's try to get a general picture of how the Christians in the communities to which he wrote tried to live.

They believed that Jesus' death and resurrection had made the world bright with promise. Jesus was in the world, transforming it, particularly through them. They experienced the power of the risen Jesus—his Spirit—within them. The Spirit opened their eyes to God's love for them and made them cry out to him ''Father, our Father!'' (Gal 4:6). To express their central belief in ''Gospel'' language, God's kingdom *was* coming at the center of their own, ordinary lives.

Jesus' Spirit gave all of them their special ability to be ''fellow workers'' of a loving and faithful God, an accessible God, who brought them fruitfulness and joy through the life of Jesus in them.

13

A GREEK SEAPORT

The first picture we have (about 50 A.D.) of such people comes to us by accident.

Paul was writing to the community he had recently founded in the seaport of Thessalonica. Their neighbors were making things rough for them by various kinds of persecution. Keeping true to Christ's moral teaching was proving difficult; and living in a Greek city—especially this major seaport—increased the problem.

News had just come to Paul that neither the persecutions of neighbors nor the sexual allurements of the city had won the day. His letter starts with a long burst of gratitude that in spite of everything they had stayed true. He goes on to urge them to continue living as a Christian community should. In such a community the members

> warned the idle, encouraged the timid, helped the weak, were
> patient with everyone. They saw that no one paid back wrong
> for wrong, but at all times made it their aim to do good to one
> another and to all people. (1 Thes 5:14–15).

Has anyone described a way of life more gentle and supportive, yet entirely down to earth? There is nothing elaborate or "pious": just practical humanity in everyday life.

And there is nothing of the self-complacent ghetto—an occupational disease, as we know, of all religions: "do good to one another *and to all people.*"

If we look more closely, we see that there are *no* second-class citizens. It's the job of everyone to take his or her part, according to ability, in the activities Paul described. Yes, of course there were leaders (5:12–13). Their task was to help all this happen. But the responsibilities of the leaders weren't to swamp those of the rest. Both the leaders and the community as a whole had full responsibility, which, like a happily-married couple, complemented each other.

1 Thessalonians gives us no more than a tantalizingly brief sketch. But a fuller picture emerged, a couple of years later, in a different Greek city.

THE JEWEL IN THE GREEK CROWN

Corinth prided itself on being the jewel in the Greek crown, and its beauty, wealth and sophistication provided grounds for the boast.

Paul's eighteen-month stay there had given him first-hand experience of how their tendencies to pride and self-centeredness could wreck their Christianity. And when he came to write 1 Corinthians, about a year after he had left them, he had heard of the problems those tendencies were causing.

What Paul does in the letter is to build so far as possible on the good things that were happening in the community and remind them what they should really be doing about them.

One result (chapters 12–14) is an extraordinarily rich job-description of a Christian—especially if we run it together with a similar piece in Romans (12:1–8). 1 Thessalonians gives us the flavor of a genuine Christian life; but here we have the inner dynamics of a Christian community. True, some parts of the Corinthian church had gotten these wrong. Some fashionable errors and their own natural weaknesses were misleading them. But we can get behind these through the letter and see what Paul believed should actually be happening when Christians live in the same street, village or city.

THE CHURCH: A COMMUNION OF COMMUNITIES

Each Christian belonged to a small group of fellow Christians—say, twenty to thirty—in their locality. They met for encouragement, prayer, teaching, support, and worship in people's homes. You thought of each other as brother or sister, not because it seemed like the correct thing to do, but because you were conscious of sharing intimately God's fellowship and life. Each Christian knew that Jesus' one command, to love, demanded that you learn to know and work with others, affirm them as the individuals they were, and receive from them, for your own strengths and weaknesses, their love and forgiveness.

Christianity was about becoming mature: about becoming ever more transformed into being, yourself, the "image" of a loving, free, creative God. And the purpose of the community was to help you in this: to support you and to challenge you.

Community arose as naturally, as spontaneously, as prayer and loving service.

If shared Christian living arose in a household, then the household was a Christian community with its own leader—maybe the head of the house—who would preside over its Eucharist.

If shared Christian living arose from a wider sense of neighborhood, then neighborhood communities arose of the size that could fit into the living rooms of the houses available.

Of course there remained the task of linking these communities with each other and with the whole Christian Church in their life and their teaching. And sometimes we know great difficulties arose. But in spite of the difficulties, a Christianity that did not basically consist of family-like communities was inconceivable. How else could you really be an embodiment for actual people of Christ's own service and love?

"DIFFERENT WAYS OF SERVING"

Of course, a community can stifle you. It can force its members into a dreary uniformity and rob them of their identity and creativity.

Christian life, for Paul, was the opposite. Both the diversity Paul takes for granted in these small, new communities, and the responsibilities he wants everyone to have, are astonishing.

Some members would contribute to the most important task of all: the understanding of what God was offering them through Jesus. Some did that more intuitively (the prophets) and some more systematically (the teachers). Each in his or her own way would say in the meetings what God seemed to be saying now to this little community. These were the people who had a special gift for giving people God's encouragement, warning or guidance—a type of person most of us perhaps have come across, not necessarily people with much formal education.

Any member might have these powers. The community's job was not to *give* these powers, or to stifle them, but to discern who God had given them to and to thank him for the light he shed in all their lives through these ordinary men and women.

Paul believed that this gift of prophecy was the highest gift (1 Cor 14:1), so long as it was correctly used to help and encourage all the others to use their own different gifts.

Some of the others would have the gift of being able to help ordinary people in some practical way, others of showing kindness to the sick or destitute, others of offering physical healing.

Then there were people with the gift of organizing and co-ordinating the overall aims of the community (much as a pastor does today).

There was the person who was good at handling finance—the Christian communities in Corinth had a wide social mix, and the city was renowned for its successful businessmen.

And to complete this extraordinarily wide range, there were

people who could contribute to the unconscious life of the community, for example by song. Each had his or her own gift, and had to use it, both in everyday life and in worship (1 Cor 14:26). Life in a Pauline community can hardly have been dull!

To anyone who wanted a tidy, predictable Christianity, this would have been a daunting array of activity and responsibility. Paul himself knew all too well the trouble it had caused. The Corinthians' experience of these powers in themselves had made some of them conceited. The ambition of these members wasn't to contribute to God's work in the world, but to preen themselves on their "spiritual" prowess. Strife and rivalries had riven the communities.

But Paul was entirely clear, in spite of all that trouble, that the gifts must be encouraged, not quenched. Paul's deepest certainty and experience of God was his gracious, effective kindness. That is what he had found, so strongly, so gladsomely, in his own life and in that of others.

ENCOURAGEMENT

Paul had found God's kindness cashed out at every stage of this life as a Christian in what he and other Christians experienced and could do. These various abilities of individual Christians were God's presence becoming tangible and fruitful in them. Did Paul or anyone have the right to resist that? No wonder Paul and his communities saw one of the main roles of any Christian as that of an encourager!

There was another important reason why each person's particular gift had to be encouraged. It was *as a body* that Christians showed Christ to the world. The Christians' sense of God in his power and goodness that flowed into their love for one another and what they did for others spoke more effectively about God's presence than any words.

But a body functions fully only when *all* the parts can function. ''The eye cannot say to the hand, 'I don't need you!' Nor
can the head say to the feet, 'Well, I don't need you!' (1 Cor
12:21). Simply to show that it was a body—not just a loose collection of human beings—each member had to play his or her own
part, and the others, leaders and all, had to help that.

EUCHARIST

It was in their Eucharists, of course, that all this found its
fullest expression.

Paul had to make clear to the Corinthians that if they weren't
really trying to be a community, it wasn't a Eucharist at all (1 Cor
11:17–34).

It seems probable that the Mass would often consist of some
prophets and teachers sharing their insights about what God was
saying today to the lives of this little community (say, in an Old
Testament reading or a letter from an apostle) and the rest responding in silent prayer, or by encouraging one another, or by
song. There was no fixed formula—there wouldn't be one for centuries. The community's sense of God in each other's everyday
lives and their hope of one day being with Jesus always was the
guiding force.

The main part of the Eucharist looked like the Last Supper.
There were real tables. You sat down together for a real meal, like
any family.

Yes, indeed, it was infinitely more than a meal: your lives
were touched, and, if you would, transformed, by God's great actions, especially those through Jesus. But, as in the Last Supper,
the proclamation of these actions wasn't sounds from a distant
world. It entered, instead, into the texture of what you naturally
did together: eating and drinking around a table as you enjoyed

and celebrated all you shared with each other: the closeness, the experiences, the common purpose.

Reflection

- Which aspects of the New Testament practice of Christianity are for you particularly attractive?
- Do you find any aspects of the New Testament Church unfamiliar or surprising? If so, can you account for that?
- You may like to compare some of the main features of Christian life in much of the early Church with Christian life as it was in the 1960's and reflect on the features of the former that you would like to see more extensively regained than has happened so far.

LIFE IN THE EARLY CHURCH	THE CHURCH IN THE EARLY 1960'S
Local community primary, though must be linked with the wider Church	The papacy tended to run the whole Church as subordinate departments
Everyone's particular gift/ ministry valued and given scope—whether full-time or not	Full-time ministries had edged the ministries of most to the margin
Local community meetings for community affairs and development, as well as worship	Community meetings almost entirely just for worship
Worship a warmly human affair, in a home, where everyone could take some active part	Worship more institutional, and in a church; the laity had a passive role

The community's main responsibility to be the *sign* and the *service* of God's rule in the world

Attention mainly on liturgy and on orthodox teaching; tendency to see Christianity as about distrusting or fleeing from the world, rather than as working with Christ to transform it (though some strong papal teaching resisted this tendency)

The whole community shared in making decisions, helped by its leader(s) in a brotherly/sisterly way

The community's responsibilities absorbed by the leader; paternalistic or autocratic kind of leadership

Leadership mainly from alongside

Leadership from above

The leader's role important: to stimulate, coordinate, correct, and to link with the wider Church

Leader became a priest (i.e., in practice, primarily concerned with liturgy); exclusively male; belonging to a separate caste ("the clergy"), with a different way of life (celibate), and tending to absorb all the main ministries.

But leaders not a separate caste, or exclusively male, and leadership tended to be shared

PART 3
TODAY

Chapter 1
The Church Rediscovering Its Heritage

A couple have been married more than twenty years. They remain friends and loyal to one another, but the warmth and joy of the first years of their marriage have slipped away, without their really noticing.

Then something happens—maybe a holiday together—and they suddenly realize what they have lost. Recapturing the depth of their relationship becomes the priority of their lives.

We Catholics today are in a similar situation. In the 1950's the great majority of us were entirely content with the way of being a Catholic we had inherited. It hardly occurred to us that change was even possible.

Then Scripture research opened up for us very different approaches, like those we have been considering. Of course, the Bible had been accessible before, but more as texts rather than as people's experience. What triggered off in our minds that we'd lost much more of our heritage was being able to enter into the lives, values and attitudes of some of the New Testament communities. If leadership in their church was bringing together *everyone's* gifts, why not in ours? If they didn't have any second-class citizens, need we?

Of course we realize that it's not a question of imitating the life-style of the early Christians—any more than that married couple would feel obliged to go back to the clothes and social customs of the year of their marriage.

So, what is basically going on in the Church today is an at-

tempt to recapture some central Christian values that understandably became obscured in the very difficult times the Church has
had to live through.

Chapter 2
The Rediscovery of Community

How *do* people acquire important new values that challenge and change their way of life?

Not simply by being told to. Instruction affects the head; but we cling to our deeper values with the heart also.

Only experience can address the heart. Somehow we have *to feel*—not just intellectually agree with—the central values the New Testament now shows us.

In a sense we rediscovered community twenty years ago. The Pope and the bishops proclaimed it at Vatican Council II (1962-1965). But community, like love, can be caught not taught. We needed to find ways of experiencing it for ourselves. Let's see how Catholics are doing that today.

GROUPS IN RENEW AND OTHER PROGRAMS

The first big wave in the rising tide I saw in Newark, New Jersey in 1980. As you go from the railroad station to the diocesan headquarters, economic depression seems to hang like a cloud over every street. Yet even in a diocese that includes wide areas like that, forty thousand people were already meeting in groups of ten to twelve every week to reflect together on Scripture. Rich and poor, black and white, had discovered that what to them as indi-

27

viduals could often seem obscure Bible texts could give meaning
to their lives if explored with other people.

Even in the New Testament, some communities were less able
to embody this fullness of life than others (cf Part IV, Chapter 5).

If these people had felt those meetings to be no more than
Bible classes, they wouldn't have kept them up for more than two
years, and there wouldn't be nearly two million Catholics imitating them in seventy dioceses around the United States. The
Church in America had never seen the like before. How can we
explain this phenomenon?

One clue may be that the founder of this program (Renew)
knew people. He had been pastor of the poorest parish in Newark.

But the main clue lies in what we've already seen in Scripture. When Christians come together to reflect on Scripture,
they're not mainly looking for instruction or information: they're
discovering Christ in what he did and in his life now in our fellow
Christians. And as we discover Christ in our midst, we find our
true selves.

No one is so naive, of course, as to expect instant success.
Discovery of another person is usually gradual.

Gradually we get accustomed to the places we meet and the
people we're beginning to share with.

If we're following Renew, we start by looking at the fact that
Christ calls each of us. The person who can, as the Son of God,
transform our world wants *me*. He loves all men and women. But
that love has to become tangible, available to people through an
ordinary flawed person like me. That, as a Christian, is the gran-
deur of my calling.

As I become more aware of this, two things are happening
to me. First, the Scripture passages we take are helping me appreciate who Jesus is and his closeness to me. It comes home to
me more and more that the whole story of our relationship is the
unfolding to me of God's effective kindness.

I see it in St. Paul and his communities. The kindness—the

"grace"—of God did not hover above them as some strange religious object. They experienced God's graciousness in the new powers within them. They no longer stood on the quicksands of fate, subject to the shifts of uncertain fortune like "those who have no hope" (1 Thes 4:13). Their whole lives were graced. Whatever happened to them, God's kindness would win if they let it be the main force in their lives.

As I get used to the group I am with and to sharing thoughts and feelings with them, I increasingly see all this happening in myself and the other members.

It may be someone in the group who has been struggling against great difficulties to be helpful to a member of his or her family. It may be someone showing, very quietly, courage, patience or joy. One way or another, our growing awareness that Christianity isn't primarily a set of notions but is about God in people opens our eyes to the biggest surprise of all: God is in *these* people! The Spirit really *"does* produce love, joy, peace, patience, kindness, goodness, faithfulness, humility and self-control" in people we're coming to know (Gal 5:22-23). As these people's life-stories begin to unfold just a little before me, I see that Jesus' creative presence (his spirit) is in them.

Jean Marie Hiesberger of Kansas City has been involved in this kind of thing for some years. "People are for the first time talking with others," she told me, "about what our faith means. The group may be Bible study or Renew. Either way, it eventually leads us into the question: What should I be doing?" We'll come to the results of that in our next chapter.

THE PARISH

"Now that's all very well," you may say, "for people in parishes where a program like Renew is running well. But what happens to us when that's not so?"

It's certainly true that many people have not so far been given this kind of opportunity, and in some parishes only a small minority gets involved in the program. So the parish is the main form of Christian life for most of us. And that remains to a large extent true even of the people we've just been talking about.

In many parishes, factors like the size or the architecture of the buildings don't encourage community. Other obstacles come from us. The pressures of work, and the appeal of our other social groups and of television, tend to make much parish involvement unattractive or very difficult. The result of all this is that for most people their main form of Christian life consists of Sunday worship, special occasions like baptisms and funerals, and occasional fund-raising for good causes.

But, as we've already partly seen, several influences are coming together to change that. Above all we are beginning to see from the New Testament that a Christian life that does not include sharing the encouragement and service of others, built on prayer and Scripture, misses so much of its richness. Dolores Leckey—whom also we'll meet again later—wasn't speaking only for herself when she said: "We need community to see Christ more completely and to reflect Christ more accurately."

People's experience of everyday life is strengthening the growing feeling that Christianity is fundamentally incomplete without community. The American bishops noted this fact in 1980. "Because lay women and men," they said, "experience intimacy, support, acceptance and availability in family life, they seek the same in their Christian communities. This is leading to a review of parish size, organization, priorities and identity. It has already led to intentional communities, basic Christian communities and some revitalized parish communities."[1]

Certainly we all know Catholics who prefer a private kind of Christianity. I know many of that kind who have a profound spirituality. But in some cases the preference for privacy may arise from other motives. Religion is for my comfort. Serving the needs of others is not a regular part of my agenda. And I will strongly resist any changes in worship or in policy that might upset me.

But for many people ''it is difficult to be a praying, caring, serving person all by oneself.''[2] Nearly ten years ago, the bishops' advisors found that ''the heart of many problems of disaffection from the Church is a loss of confidence in the Church as an apt structure for significant human community.''[3]

HOW CAN THE PARISH BECOME A COMMUNITY?

How is the church going to be able to make possible what many of its members want?

On one side we have people's experience of intimacy and support in family life and their growing perception that New Testament Christianity is stunted without that. On the other side, we have the pressures of modern life and the majority's lack of experience of ''community'' Christianity, largely because of the size of the modern parish.

The stakes are very high. Our *need* of a Catholic Church that is fully alive is so great, but it is only in the context of a community church that most of us effectively ask the question ''What should I be doing?'' Until most of us ask that question, the church will largely sleep.

So what can be done?

It is largely a matter of building on our experience of Christian community and of using Scripture to help us appreciate more richly what we find there.

In most parishes a lot of people, as we know, already get together for such things as sport, picking up children from school, and helping to run parish socials. What many parishes are doing is to build on that kind of natural clustering.

Thomas Sweetser describes one way in which a parish did

that. It knew that the same people were regularly coming to its Sunday family Mass. It invited "families to help plan the liturgy and in this way provided a feeling of belonging and closeness. Family groups came together two weeks in advance to pray over the readings and plan the liturgy. The groups then contacted other families to help with the Mass by constructing a banner based on the theme, by doing the readings as a family, by bringing up the gifts, or by choosing the songs. Groups of families experienced a sense of solidarity as they worked together to plan the Mass and join in the celebration."[4]

Of course Catholics share many other kinds of interests than worship. We appreciate the companionship and the support of working at our interests with others, in spite of the demands that is bound to make on us.

The shared interest may be that of parents for school children, of single parents, or of the divorced/separated. Another kind of interest is something a group would like to do for people in the parish or neighborhood. For generations, for example, some groups have worked to help the poor. Others may run events that bring together ethnic groups, help the elderly, the sick, or the lonely, seek and welcome newcomers to the parish, or focus on a social problem in the area.

All these can be good foundations. But somehow the parish has to find ways to build on them. Full Christian community only occurs if what we are sharing with others is reflected on prayerfully in the light of Scripture and if it leads to service for others. "A parish is not a place where, but a people who," wrote the bishop of Arlington, Virginia to his diocese in 1984. Maybe in Arlington. But it doesn't happen anywhere without a great deal of work.

The first thing, obviously, is to recognize who the men and women who might become more fully a community really are, and what they can do. So the next chapter will look at how we are recapturing the conviction that *all* are called to take an active part of some kind in Christian life, and the directions in which this is taking us.

Chapter 4 will consider how we're learning to work as a team. Then, in Chapter 5, we shall turn to the leader of all this: the man who has to bear the brunt of so much change which, as a young priest, he very likely never bargained for.

When we have looked carefully, in this way, at the main directions in today's Church, we should be able to get some kind of idea of the developments we should seek for tomorrow's.

Reflection

- Have you had experience of some kind of Christian group? If so, what did it show you about yourself, about God, and about other people?
- Do you think that most of us may need the support and encouragement of a Christian group to help us seriously tackle the question: "What should I be doing?"
- Do you agree that "we need community to see Christ more completely and to reflect Christ more accurately"? If so, is your parish adequately supplying that need? What makes it difficult for a parish to supply that need, and how can the difficulties be diminished?

"Sunday Mass is not enough for a vital Christianity. Small communities flow from the Gospel, the Catholic understanding of community, the need privatized Americans have for brotherhood and sisterhood found in spiritual intimacy and social action." (Dennis Geaney, O.S.A., 1985)[5]

- This view is based on a wide experience of the American scene. How far do you agree with it?

Chapter 3
Who Does What?

Who does what in your parish?

When we go to the Sunday Mass, we see lay people taking important parts in the service. Men and women are readers, give Communion, and take Communion to the sick. Not so long ago it was unthinkable for any but clergy to perform these functions.

Then there are the key roles taken by lay people outside the Mass. There will probably be members of the parish council and the religious education coordinator. If your parish is following RCIA, lay people will be officially teaching the faith. In many parishes that's only the beginning.

IMPLICATIONS

The New Testament makes clear why all this is happening. It shows that Christianity is about *the transformation of the world*, and that this happens through *each* Christian using his or her gifts in loving service.

The way we experience and grow in intimacy with Christ is by thinking, feeling and working with him. Can intimacy between persons grow in any other way? In order to understand the implications of all this today, it is useful to recall what happens when a Christian undertakes any ministry:

1. The first has to do with Jesus' resurrection itself, where the full creative power of God became present in a human person. Because of the resurrection, that power is potentially in the whole human race. As Christians we especially have *Jesus' power, or Spirit, in us*. This happens—if we permit—in the specific gifts he gives us. Just now I *hope* I have some gift of writing!

2. The second element is that *we come to know God's graciousness* because we experience being *graced* by it. My experience of using the talent God has given me as I take my part in the work of the kingdom makes me aware of God's kindness and the fruitfulness of his presence in me. The stories of Jesus and of Paul are pervaded with a mood of joyful, and calculated, celebration. Even in the shadow of probable execution, Paul could say: "Don't worry about anything. Always be joyful" (Phil 4:4-5).

3. The third element is that my talent *will have effect*, because it is *God's work* I have joined.

4. Work can be impersonal or mechanical; but God's work is always that of *loving service*. We think of the way Jesus noticed people's needs, his kindly, practical compassion, the joy and support of his friendship. We think, too, of how people have served us—where the smile has sometimes spoken more strongly than many actions.

These four elements are present in the life of *any* sincere Christian. They, in their own specific way, share in the power by which Christ transforms the world (his Spirit). In that sharing they experience God's gracious kindness; they see God strongly active in the world, and all this takes place in loving service of others.

This is the New Testament portrait of *every* Christian—not just the ones with official functions. When Jesus talked about talents, he didn't mean just his chief disciples. When Paul talked about special gifts for service, he wasn't thinking just of prominent people like teachers and prophets. Some of the Corinthians thought that only top people had talents, and that they could use them for their own gratification. Paul replies to them, in effect:

"You're wrong. *Everyone* has a talent. Everyone's talent is important. Use yours for the work of Christ's 'body' where you live. And use it in love. Then your life will come to a more complete fulfillment than any of us can dream" (1 Cor 12–14). St. Peter put the matter succinctly: "Each one, as a good manager of God's different gifts, must use for the good of others the special gift he has received from God" (1 Pet 4:10).

IMPLICATIONS OF ADULTHOOD

But *how* should we use our special gift? Like mere operators docilely waiting for the nod of our masters?

Pope Pius X, in 1906, said that in the Church there are two different classes of person: "There are the members of the various orders of the hierarchy and the multitude of believers. . . . The duty of the multitude is to permit themselves to be ruled and to follow obediently the directives of the officeholders."

But Scripture has shown that *all* are called to be mature and responsible partners—not just "the orders of the hierarchy." Paul goes out of his way to stress that *each* of us must act as a member of Christ's body, and that in a body the less imposing functions are as necessary as any other.

An adult role in the Church, the American bishops said in 1980, flows from something all of us have: baptism and confirmation. They went on to describe what this means in the American church of today: "One of the chief characteristics of lay men and women today is their growing sense of being adult members of the Church. Adulthood implies knowledge, experience and awareness, freedom and responsibility, and mutuality in relationships. It is true that the experience of lay persons as 'church members' has not always reflected this understanding of adulthood. Now, thanks to Vatican II, lay women and men feel themselves called to exercise the same mature interdependence and practical self-direction which characterizes them in other areas of life.''[1]

All this shows us what a parish has. It hasn't got a priest, a team, some liturgical ministers, and the rest as "patients" to be tended with church services, moral teaching, and social functions. It has got a large number of people, each of them graced with his or her special talent, and each called to use that "with mature interdependence and practical self-direction." The priest and his team are no longer a select ensemble, with the rest mainly audience. They are the conductors of an orchestra, so that the music of God's good news can be heard.

Some people deduce from all this that we are sinking into a formless democracy, with the pastor "reduced to the ranks." When we look at the pastor's role in Chapter 5, we shall see, I think, that though this fear is quite natural for the older of us, it is groundless. We shall see that the pastor's role is, in fact, very much enhanced. But for the moment let's look more closely at the "orchestra" the pastor is asked to conduct. Who is doing what?

GOING PUBLIC

Most people, of course, are getting on with their family lives and their jobs. Who shares more fully in Christ's costly loving kindness than the mother and father who cope with love and even humor with night after night of a squalling infant, or with the long journey of an adolescent son or daughter toward adulthood? Quite often there have been long-term difficulties to overcome. It may be strong differences in the couple's temperaments. Or it may be a single parent having somehow to be "two." Even so, the family's faith in Christ helps them to "minister" to each other's needs with love and confidence. Their family is a place where the members experience support and encouragement. They are making Christian community.

All this, of course, is an essential part of Christian ministry. The way I choose to act among those whose daily lives I share obviously makes me the kind of person I am.

But in the synagogue in Nazareth Jesus didn't just announce that he was going to help people. He told his amazed fellow townsfolk that in his giving sight to the blind and freedom to captives, they should recognize *that God now ruled*! In the last resort, the world is *not* ruled by aimlessness or chaos, nor by evil, but by the God of faithfulness and compassion.

He would indeed offer love to everyone, freely, merrily and increasingly with lethal danger. As he saw individuals in their need he was moved with compassion. But it was also the family— the human family—for which he had that compassion. His service to that family was to help them recognize in his compassion the presence, the personality, of the Lord of all life.

A Christian is someone who continues that today. He or she is a member of God's people, who, with Jesus, is chosen to *proclaim* "the wonderful acts of God, who called you out of darkness into his own marvelous light" (1 Pet 4:9). If I do not wish to join Christ in his work, I cannot really say I want to know Christ. As an individual, and as a member of my local church, I am called to "go public" as my gifts and opportunities allow me.

Readers with exceptionally fine memories will remember me mentioning early in this book the pastor of Elk Grove Village, Illinois. He told his parishioners: "Our business is the reign of God; and our strategy, the only way we will achieve it, is the inner spiritual conversion of all men and women to God in Christ Jesus."

He presented that—you may remember—as a practical proposition. It could only be done if the parishioners were willing to pool their different talents. "At the end of five years I expect every person in this area will have been touched in some way" by the prayers and actions of the parishioners, like mailings, advertisements, home visits, block parties, receptions, classes, ecumenical projects and so on.

Of course there are no blueprints. Many other American parishes, as we shall see, are adopting similar strategies, but every group of people and every neighborhood is different.

Elk Grove Village is mentioned here because it shows the kind of thing Christian ministry is concerned with. It's *not* the work of the few—*every* baptized person is called to it. It does *not* primarily have to do with religious services—though these are essential for its nourishment. It arises from the fact that *our business is the same as Christ's: the rule of God coming to the world.* And it happens in our neighborhood by each of us using our particular gift, whether that's sorting out a mailing, helping with a reception, giving a class, or offering a warm welcome.

There are other equally important ways in which we can stand for the kingdom. As a local Christian community we can help to free people from the "captivity" of injustice and deprivation. As individuals with (if we're lucky) a job, we can let Christ illuminate and give full significance to that part of our lives as well. Later we'll consider the immense possibilities in both of these new avenues of exploration. But, first, what general picture of Christian ministry in your or my neighborhood is beginning to emerge?

"IT IS PEOPLE WHO COUNT"

One conclusion that we can certainly *not* draw is that all of us should seek appointment to some official ministry. It was one of the pioneers in this field, the bishop of Kansas City, Missouri, who stressed not long ago that though "everyone must be a minister, in today's Church we have and need both informal and formal ministry."² Thousands of Catholics feel no call to be a Reader, a Eucharistic minister or a Youth Counselor. But all of us can minister informally to the people we meet by "talking Jesus" from time to time, voting by our conscience, and consciously letting our Christianity color our relationships with our fellow workers and friends.

Rosemary Haughton recalled from her own experience how *whole families* exercise informal ministry. You find such families, she said, in every neighborhood in the country. They have a gift for hospitality. They watch out for others and support them. They help prepare the young for marriage, support those caught in troubled marriages, and hold out a helping hand to families in need.

All these people are giving evidence that God's gracious kindness is here. They constitute most of what a parish "has." The role of the counselors, the readers and the other formal ministers is to give scope, encouragement and support to all these people.

In 1980 the Archbishop of Milwaukee described the primary aim of the Church as "the development of the contribution of each member." "In other words," he explained, "the well-being, growth and gift of each baptized member should become the object of the concern of all. It is people who count."³

A year later the American Bishops' Committee on Parish Life pointed to the other side of that coin: "Too often forgotten is . . . that without encouragement the call to a life of church ministry could well go unheeded, leaving parishes without the leadership they need."⁴

Reflection

- Among the people you know, which individuals or families particularly impress you by the informal ministry they exercise?
- Would more support and encouragement be helpful for such people? If so, what should be done to help them?

FORMAL MINISTRIES

Let's see how these new perspectives are helping us to understand the real importance of the formal ministries. We can take some of the more familiar.

Ministry of the Reader

It will take some time for us all to say "goodbye" to the feeling that ministry happens mainly in church, and that there it consists of going through prescribed words and actions. But it does help to remember that the reader at Mass was originally involved in teaching and explaining the Scripture passages as well as reading them.

We know that God's word is not fruitful in us unless we perceive its relevance to the situations we have to face. Does this support the view that the person "best suited to be reader is the one most involved in secular affairs"? Bear in mind that in 1972 the German bishops' request to Rome for qualified lay men and women to be commissioned to preach was accepted. The New Testament gives no warrant for believing that every person with the gift of Christian leadership is also given the gift of preaching!

We may not yet have the answers to the questions just raised, but statistics leave us in no doubt of the importance of finding them. A 1984 survey showed that the second largest cause of Catholics leaving the Church today is linked to ineffective preaching of the word of God.

Acolyte

Another example of how our better understanding of the ministry could change our practice has to do with that of acolyte. In

1976 an Italian bishop asked his brother bishops this question: Since there ought to be a connection between the service a minister performs in worship and that which he or she offers in daily life, and since one of the primary tasks of an acolyte is to bring Communion to the sick, should a person appointed to this office be well known for his or her concern for the sick? A woman is not at present permitted to be an acolyte, but she can fulfill that role as a eucharistic minister. The difference is that she cannot be ordained (cf Part 4, Chapter 5).

Usher

Other developments in worship ministries are more obvious. Who has not seen, in some parish or other, an usher performing that task like a stiff sergeant-major? The word ''usher'' may be a contributing factor. Fortunately the task is now widely seen as part of the ministry of welcome and hospitality—a ministry written deep in the New Testament. Here is how an American pastor describes this ministry:

> Ushers are greeters. The major concern of the Usher should be to welcome people, help them to find a seat, and serve their personal needs so as to facilitate their worship and exemplify that the Lord comes in relationships.[5]

When, in 1984, 320 people from the diocese of Nottingham, England came together for its assembly, they asserted their feeling that ''we neglect the Mass as a great opportunity for extending welcome.'' They wanted someone at the Sunday Mass with no other duties than ''to offer a cheerful welcome and to put people at ease within the house of God.''[6]

The ministries, therefore, connected with worship are increasingly extending beyond the bounds of worship. We better appreciate today that worship isn't the exclusive sphere where ''real religion'' takes place. Worship should affirm, celebrate, and organically grow from our lives, like the sexual act from marriage.

WE ARE ADVANCING

Some very heartening consequences of all this are becoming obvious in many places.

One is that ministry is recovering its human face. Instead of seeming distant and supranatural, it is seen to hinge, like Jesus' own ministry in the Gospels, on the quality of the relationship between the servant and the served. "Real ministry," wrote a theologian recently, "demands sensitivity: how sin and grace has touched this individual."[7]

Another heartening consequence is that we are moving from regiment toward family. Instead of being divided into two categories of the upper "class" who *give*, and the lower "class" who *receive*, we are coming to realize that we all need to do *both* those things.

Besides that, we are beginning to perceive, with Paul, that Christ abolished even the deepest known divisions between us, because the unity of God is reflected in the unity of humankind (Rom 3:30). We have moved *some* way toward men sharing in the church with women, white with black, pastor with parishioners. We've made some small beginnings with an indispensable journey. These are, of course, major growth points for today and tomorrow, which we shall explore later in this book.

However urgent that growth, we can say that our answers to "who does what in your parish?" are likely to be very different to the ones we would have given just a few years ago. Almost half the Catholics who are in regular contact with the parish take part in one or more parish activities beyond religious rites.

The great majority of Catholics are content that the parish

activities are widely shared. The relatively new phenomenon of women performing ministries in the sanctuary is no exception. Eighty percent of regularly attending Catholics either welcome or have adjusted to this development.

We can surely be glad that the giftedness of so many people is being encouraged to grow and bear fruit, often for the good of many others. Later we shall see what is being done to increase our awareness of the need to proclaim God's kingdom and so to make our use of our gifts less inward-looking.

But a Christian community is called to be more than a school for the encouragement of its members' gifts. It is called to be a body—Christ's body, present and accessible in this locality. It should be an *adult, reponsible body*. Our next chapter considers the steps that are being taken in many parishes to make it that.

Reflection

- Which of the ministries being exercised in your parish do you react to most positively? What do you find to be particularly valuable in them?
- Which ministry are you already exercising or might feel drawn to? What needs in your parish does this ministry serve? How can it best be carried out in "mature interdependence"?
- How important do you think, in a parish, is "the development of the contribution of each member"? How can this be done?

Chapter 4
Sharing Responsibility

WE'RE GETTING THERE

"If a major purpose of Vatican II was to reinstate the sense that all Christians are responsible for the corporate life of the Church in the local parish, Vatican II is succeeding." On this upbeat note of optimism, the 1984–1988 Notre Dame study of Catholic parish life begins its report.

That survey's statistics are eloquent. Beyond the parish pastor, eighty-three percent of the leadership within Catholic parishes in the United States are laypersons, and seventy-five percent of the parishes currently have parish councils.

But *at what level* of leadership are laypersons participating? Are they taking a part in the important decisions? To what extent are they a clique around the pastor, while the other parishioners remain largely passive?

To answer those important questions, may I begin with a brief diversion to a lovely city?

NOT TOO FAST

Brisbane, Australia, not only brings happy memories of its beauty, but it also offers the historical perspective which we need when considering rapid change.

It is blessed by having one of the world's best bishops, and particularly since 1975, he has worked hard to involve lay people. Most of his initiatives have been most successful, and he particularly wanted good parish councils as a major means of involving lay people in parish leadership. Yet of the one hundred and sixteen parishes, only fifty percent had parish councils by 1984, and at least half of those were ineffective. Even less success was acknowledged in 1984 in almost all the English dioceses. Does this suggest that we shouldn't expect too much too suddenly?

Americans, it is true, are generally more willing to be "joiners" than Australians or the English. But even in America there are major obstacles.

It was in another fair city, Boston, Massachussetts, that one of the chief current obstacles was made clear to me. The Paulist Project there consists of a professional team with experience of developing parishes throughout the United States. They have found that many people are prevented from being maturely involved in any formal ministry because of the centuries of "parent-child" relationships between clergy and laity we have inherited. True, we have gone a long way toward understanding things better. But inherited attitudes tend to linger in our half-considered expectations and emotions long after our minds have disowned them.

A lay person, therefore, who becomes a reader, a member of a parish council, or whatever, can subconsciously need stronger affirmation from the pastor than is needed in most adult partnerships. The pastor is often unaware of that, and the result is either discouragement or the wrong kind of assertiveness.

The pastor, too, can be unconsciously acting in paternalistic ways which might horrify him if he were conscious of them.

If lay ministry is going to come to maturity in the Church, this inherited obstacle will have to be dismantled. Theology cannot regularly achieve that unaided. We all need to check on our attitudes.

I think, too, of the other reasons why pastors don't have genuine responsibility with lay people.

There is the sheer busyness of most pastors. Thirty years ago, most of their job, including liturgy, was routine. It seemed to need no special skills, no sharing leadership with others (not even with the curates!) and no personal creativity.

Today a pastor need skills in counseling and communication. He is expected to share his tasks with a number of committees and bring personal input to liturgy. He has less clergy to help him, on average he is older, and there are more Catholics. Worst of all, when he sees so many of the functions formerly reserved to him entrusted to lay people, he may be uncertain of the identity of his role.

Amidst this busyness, complexity, and maybe self-doubt, it's not so surprising that many pastors pay lip-service to lay participation. "Ah yes, we'll have a parish council, because people expect that. But important decisions will have to be mine."

Unfortunately statistics show that this attitude is widespread. Yes, seventy-five percent of the parishes have councils. But only four percent of pastors identify the parish council as one of the five most important factors contributing to parish life.

Despair, however, is unnecessary! In the last few years we are seeing the emergence of something very different. Church law and mature experience are beginning to produce a kind of parish council which can develop the parish into what it is meant to be. As this gathers momentum in the next few years, what will we increasingly see?

HELP FROM THE BISHOPS

Consider the reality of the average American parish. More than forty percent of the parishes serve over twenty-five hundred people, and sixty-five percent are in suburbs or cities. It is in *this* kind of context that the primary aim of the Church has somehow to take effect: the development of the contribution of each member.

Of course the problem can't be reduced to that of simply supplying a piece of encouragement to over twenty-five hundred people, the way you might supply ignition keys to a fleet of automobiles already set to go! We need to use our gifts *as Christ's body*. And we need to use them *for others*. For recovering these essential dimensions, we all need a great deal of help.

One major help in tackling this problem is the strong message from the bishops that solving it is very important and that the body that needs to do that is the parish council.

They have put forward a new standard of measurement of leadership in the pastor and the parish council. Successful leadership:

- clearly articulates what God is calling this parish to do;
- invites and supports the many gifts that the Spirit has provided within the parish community. This will "effectively animate the leadership of others."

The most promising way to do this is to:

- encourage the fullest possible collaboration of clergy, religious and laity "through participation in the decision-making process, as well as in the various ministries;"
- develop in the parish the correct understanding of the parish's vocation.

In other words the parish council should help the parish be a body of gifted people and help it to use its gifts effectively for others. It offers the parish coordination and wisdom.

One result of this clear lead is to put the various activities of the parish in their true perspective. If that isn't done, money and maintenance are likely to become the front-runners in its agenda, and the parish will miss its real purpose. It will have no deep relevance to the lives of the rest of the parishioners.

How different if the parish council is "the backbone of parish life and of all the ministries as planner and unifier," to quote one bishop. Then it has a goal which we can all deeply relate to. Each of us can feel we have an important contribution to make to it!

Yes, parish councils *can* help.

Now we've seen that ninety-six percent of pastors don't see their parish councils as anything like that. But the tide is turning. The good news is that some dioceses are helping their parishes to have such councils. What steps are they taking to achieve that?

The first step is to give them real power. "In union with the pastor the council is the decision-making body" in the parish. It's true that Church law makes it only consultative. But when people are truly brothers and sisters in Christ, they listen to each other and trust them. "Within the context of the faith community, consultation has its own authority," Cardinal Bernard Law pointed out to his priests when talking to them about parish councils in Boston.

The next step is to help the members use their power well. They have the task of helping the parish to discern how they should use their gifts and listen to the needs of all. None of us can do that without help. We need training, and we need to approach our task in a spirit of prayerful listening. So prayer and reflection are being prescribed as the best opening to every meeting.

It's easy to see that this must be the key to the whole process. A parish council isn't there to hand out decisions like a telex. It's there to respond to the presence of God in a community of people as they try to work with him for his kingdom. If it shows responsiveness, openness and trust, its influence will be so much greater.

The third step is, of course, to start getting the parish involved. Every parishioner has his or her own gift and interest, but is quite likely to have grown up in a church where there was no incentive to think about using it. Each of us *could* cry out with the same gratitude as Paul's: "By God's generosity I am what I am, and the gift he gave me was not without effect" (1 Cor 15:10)— *but only if we're made to feel wanted.*

This is how some parishes—like those in the diocese of Milwaukee—try to make everyone feel wanted. A list is made of what needs to be done in the parish. There is:

- prayer and worship
- Christian development of each person in his or her present situation (family person, single, youth, premarried, "hurting" family);
- Christian service (works of charity; advocating for people who are hurting or for change in public policies that hurt people—especially the more vulnerable);
- parish renewal (building community in the parish; welcoming; helping the parish reach out to others);
- building and finance

When you lay out the tasks like that, people can come to realize two important things. First, those tasks can't all be done by the pastor, or even by the parish council; second, there's a slot there for everyone! Each parish needs good welcomers, people handy with buildings, people with experience of needs or injustices in the neighborhood—to mention but a few. Then of course there's also need for more specialized helpers, like those who can help with alcoholic dependency, and experts in finance or marriage counseling or music. Looking at the list brings it home to many of us that if Christ's work is to be done in our community, each one of us may have to take our part.

In Milwaukee everyone is encouraged to join the parish committee corresponding to her or his talent. Of course it takes patience, time, and skill to get these committees going. But the rewards are found to be very great. Participation in a Christian group that keeps quietly remembering that Christ is present in its midst is a deep experience.

ENCOURAGING AND COORDINATING

As this begins to happen, the committees will need help to ensure that they work together. That will need organization: meetings and the rest. But the key element is a *spirit of trust and co-operation*. These people's growing experience of work for the kingdom—say, in helping the sick, the poor, or an oppressed person, or making the young or newcomers feel welcome—will make them see that their work is important. But our growing enthusiasm for our work can cause rivalry with other bodies or a feeling of lack of appreciation from them. Therefore much of the parish council's job is to generate a feeling that we are Christian sisters and brothers who trust and value each other. I will listen as well as speak, and I won't pretend that *I* have all the answers.

So far, then, the parish council has:

- divided the parish's main tasks into groups/committees;
- taken practical steps to encourage everyone to get involved;
- tried to generate a sense of our being a team.

The groups are by now working at their activities. They are finding people's real needs, trying to meet them as a body of Christians and integrating their work with that of the other groups and with the parish's life and worship.

Will their efforts adequately reflect the depth and significance of the life within them? Will they really work with Christ as he reaches out in love to others in the power of his resurrection?

The hard work often shown by these groups may impel us to answer: "Of course."

THE PEOPLE AROUND

Unfortunately, we cannot count on that. The life of Christ is so incredibly rich, as he tries to reach out to *all* men and women in the complexity of their actual lives as loved individuals, that it's easy for us to settle for something less than *love* or something less than the *human reality* that Christ wants to reach through us.

Take my friend Bob. He's been a devoted member of his parish for more than fifty years. Everyone knows him as kindly and intelligent. A few months ago he was showing me around the city where he has been living all those years. As we were talking, I asked him whether there were many poor people living there.

"Poor people?" he asked—trying to see the relevance of what he obviously regarded as a mighty odd question! "I don't know," he said doubtfully, "I haven't *seen* any."

Of course preachers had reminded him year after year about Jesus' preference for the poor, but somehow it had never become an important part of his outlook as a Christian.

Most American Catholics, like Bob, are middle class. It's difficult to have much interest in people we never see. Yet fifteen percent of Americans are poor—two-fifths of them children. Forty percent of the American poor get no welfare, no food stamps, no public housing, no medicaid, no school lunches.

That is only one of the elements that can easily be overlooked. Others are the lack of welcome that ethnic minorities often feel in our middle class parishes, and the role of the local church in doing something about social injustice in the neighborhood and proclaiming the Kingdom to others. Statistics show that otherwise excellent parishes are often blind to these.

A parish council's task is to help the parish see its activities in the light of *Jesus'* priorities. "Yes, these activities are fine," it says to the committee. "But are they pulling in different directions? And are they sufficiently set on the paths that the Gospels tell us we need to travel? Maybe the answer to both questions is a resounding 'yes.' But our job is to help you keep the parish's activity set on Christ's goals."

It is certainly true that, in this matter of sharing responsibility, progress is being made. Most parishes do have parish councils, even though, so far, mostly with a low level of sharing in important decision-making.

But awareness is growing about the route we should go, and about the obstacles that can impede our progress. Dioceses like Milwaukee can make available experiences of successful journeys being made.

On foundations like these, maybe all of us can soon advance. The parish of the future could have the characteristics of adulthood: sharing, relevance, and fulfilling work that would be the envy and admiration of many.

Reflection

1. Parish Community

"The primary aim of the Catholic Church in the United States should not be simply to multiply ministries for their own sake, but to renew and strengthen church communities." (U.S. Bishops' National Advisory Council)

- What are the main ways in which your own parish community is being renewed and strengthened?
- Which of these ways do you find most helpful: for yourself? for the people you know well?
- How far does your parish council serve to renew and strengthen the parish? Have you any suggestions about how it could do that better?

2. The Community's Participation

"The parish leadership develops the appropriate structures which will allow for participation in the decision-making process, as well as in the various ministries of the parish, including those of worship, service, education, formation and evangelization. . . . The parish council remains the most promising way to make sure such participation occurs." (U.S. Bishops' Committee on the Parish, 1981)

- To what extent has such participation been achieved so far in your own parish? In what areas of participation do you find your parish strongest?
- Are there any weaknesses that can't be altogether explained by the fact that we're at an early stage? How could such weaknesses perhaps be overcome?
- How effective is your parish council in making sure such participation occurs? Do you know of any ways in which it could become more effective for that purpose?

3. The Parish Council

"The parish council has very clear functions: to develop the correct understanding of the parish's mission and to formulate policies so that the necessary directions are taken if the mission is to be carried out." (U.S. Bishops' Committee on the Parish)

- How is your parish council fulfilling these functions?
- What has been the effect on the life of the parish of the main activities of your parish council? How could this effectiveness be increased?
- "A parish could establish its goals for the coming year and miss the whole area of social justice because the majority of parishioners, or at least the more articulate ones, do not feel that this is an important aspect of being a parish community" (Thomas Sweetser, *Successful Parishes*, p. 98). Is there a danger of this in your parish? This book considers social justice in parishes in Part IV, Chapter 3.

Chapter 5
The Pastor

TODAY'S OPPORTUNITIES

The great developments we have just been following obviously cannot happen in a parish without the leadership of the pastor. In the bringing to birth in our time of this profoundly richer Church, he is in most cases the indispensable midwife.

We have already touched on some of the things that can prevent that, and we must return to them a little later. But if we're going to get the contemporary situation in the right perspective, we ought to give the chief place to the opportunities. Several things have happened to make it much more possible for the pastor to be that good midwife.

The main help comes from the fact that the pastor's principal field is no longer seen as the sacristy. In 1971, the bishops of Germany, Austria and Switzerland spelled this out: "Vatican II made a decisive step forward. No longer was (the priest) presented principally as the 'man of the Sacrament.' His primary task is announcing the Gospel, provided this is understood in its fullest sense . . . the whole work of bringing salvation to people in the material and social dimension in which they actually live." We'll explore what this means concretely presently. But already we can see that New Testament perspectives are beginning to return!

Of course "bringing salvation to people in the material and social dimension" of their lives is also the primary task of *every*

Christian. It is to provide scope for us all to do that that the parish exists. The uniqueness of the pastor's role is to provide this scope *as the ordained leader.*

We know that a pastor is also unique in alone being empowered to preside over the Eucharist. But he's not, as we've just seen, principally "the man of the Sacrament." His identity, his purpose is to be *the ordained leader of a group that brings the good news to people.* It is because the Eucharist is so intimately related to this purpose that he alone presides over the Eucharist.

LEADER

The pastor's job is to find ways of opening up for us the New Testament avenues along which we can know and work with Christ (through community, appreciating our gifts, working for the kingdom, and worship). His success is measured by the extent to which he can harness the many gifts in the parish to bring this knowledge of Christ into our minds and our hearts, so that Christ's values and approach to life are deeply ours.

He is "the foremost leader of the parish,"[1] but *that leadership should be shared.* We have already seen that this is the message of the New Testament. The American bishops applied that to the realities of our time (e.g., the fact that most Americans are educated), when they said that a pastor's leadership "is greatly enhanced when it continually develops the skills and structures that invite open dialogue, shared decision-making and effective action."[2]

What we have just seen about parish councils helps us understand the kind of leadership required. The parishioners as individuals need to come to believe that Jesus' Spirit *is* in each of them, that all of them *are* graced with a talent through that Spirit, and that loving service of others through that grace and that talent is the only route to fruitfulness.

Only so far as that belief is strong and deep will the parish be a community of Christians. The good pastor begins by using all the means available to strengthen that belief.

Of course he knows that his say-so by itself is not enough. People need evidence, in their own lives or those of their friends. When I see a friend coming to recognize and use a talent and being enriched by the experience of being "graced" by God and of serving others, then the teaching that *I* am gifted begins to say something to me.

And that is exactly what is happening in many American parishes. It may be in RCIA, where we see people whom we always thought of as quite "ordinary" leading others toward a commitment to the faith as sponsors or catechists. In Brisbane they described the result of RCIA in the diocese's parishes as "an explosion of ministries." People get a taste of what this "giftedness" may be about, and they want more: a young sponsor or catechist this year, maybe a youth minister next, a married sponsor or catechist this year, maybe some kind of family ministry next. In a parish I visited in Kansas City, they had to turn people away from ministries because of RCIA: they just couldn't find the means of using so many!

Renew, as we've seen, also leads parishioners in a similar direction. The two programs admirably complement one another.

Of course success is never automatic! Parishes that simply go through the routine of a program naturally achieve very little. The whole point of such methods is to try to open out for us the reality of God, ourselves and the world, and how could that happen extensively without good leadership?

A great part of the pastor's leadership, in this matter of people's gifts, lies in his relationship with people. Fundamental, of course, is his own deep conviction that the Spirit *is* in these people. If he isn't really fired by that conviction—arising from and expressed in prayer—he is either simply boring, or at most admired as a kindly but superficial manager.

If he *does* have that conviction, then his task is to communicate it to these particular people. He has to bear in mind, as we've seen, that centuries of expecting the pastor to be "father" and the parishioners to be "children" makes that communication more difficult.

Warmth and encouragement will therefore be necessary, but so also will trust. A parent is warm and encouraging to children, but adults who are genuinely partners trust one another and depend on each other's responsibility and skills.

What the good pastor is doing is trying to provide the framework and an essential part of the stimulus for the birth of a "gifted," Spirit-led Christian people. That fact that he *shares* his leadership and responsibilities does not make him any less the lynchpin of the enterprise.

LEADER OF WORSHIP

Preaching and worship are obviously central to any Christian community. We need to express what we feel and believe about the God we are discovering together in our lives.

Here, again, there are both opportunities and difficulties.

Perhaps the main *opportunity* is that most of us are trying to move from an understanding of worship as a rite which the priest was expected to perform quite mechanically to a sense that this particular community is celebrating the life of Christ that we have and share.

On the *debit* side we have a liturgy that is mainly words—with insufficient room for the imagination and for movement; the words themselves are often colorless—a kind of bland internationalese, quite unsuitable for ritual and celebration; finally, the size of many parishes makes it difficult for it to *be* a community celebration, and parishes' initiatives are made more difficult by particularly rigid Church laws in this field. Probably most of us have seen parishes work wonders even in these circumstances. But of course these difficulties take their toll.

The direction in which we need to go has been described by the bishops. "Parish preaching and worship are designed to express the incarnation of God's life in human life. This happens when it conveys discerning empathy with people's experiences (and) when people are given the opportunity to take part in developing and planning their worship."[3] But to what extent *can* the worship of most parishes express the incarnation of God's life in that community's life, or express discerning empathy with people's experiences, when there is a congregation of well over two hundred?

THE ORDAINED LEADER

Now the pastor is not just the foremost leader of the parish; he is also its *ordained* leader.

Even today, ordination is still sometimes understood in a magical way. A bishop sends a young man to a seminary for some years and then, on his ordination day, gives him the gift of leading a Christian community. Here ordination is *the bishop* giving power.

The New Testament makes it clear that it is only *the Spirit* who can give such power. The bishop, with the community, has to discern whether a person who feels called to this kind of leadership really has this gift and whether the person would be suitable for *this* community. Through the ordination ceremony the bishop affirms that gift in that person and commissions the person to use it publicly and regularly for the local church's work.

"Ordain" has to do with order, right relationship, between a rich variety of activities that happpen through and around a local church. As an officially commissioned leader, the pastor should relate the local community to the *diocese* and to the *universal* Church, who have discerned and affirmed the pastor's gift and suitability and to the *world*, as a publicly authorized leader, as well as the *members to one another*.

The New Testament has made it possible for us to rediscover the prime importance of the local church. A parish is not one of a series of chain stores, identical to the others, and programmed like a machine from headquarters. It is the place where the chief wealth of the Church—the gifts of its members—are nurtured, and where for the most part they have the best chance of being used for the world's transformation.

But the local church is such only *as part of the whole people of God*. It needs to be in mutual relationship with the diocese and with the Pope. The ordained person symbolizes and gives effect to that relationship. "Unless we truly live as the people of God, we will not be much of a sign (of God's kingdom) to ourselves or to the world."[4]

The pastor, therefore, is both the focal point of the community's quest for holiness and life service, and also the main link with the fellowship and support of the diocese.

Reflection

"This non-separation, this desire to be close to all and to share with them, is a requirement of the very vocation of the priest. It is this requirement that has been the directing force in the whole evolution that we have seen in the ministry and the life of priests, both before and after Vatican Council II." (Cardinal Marty of Paris, 1984)

- What experience have you had of this "evolution"? How valuable do you think it has been? In what ways do you think it could usefully be taken further?

"Our main concern should be the enduring gift of the Spirit among those who come together to live the Gospel." (C. Duquoc O.P., 1982)

- If the pastor's role is seen from this viewpoint, how important is it, particularly today?

"As increasing numbers of the laity are introduced into the ministerial life of the Church, some priests are haunted by the anticipated diminishment of the ministry to that of a 'sacramental functionary.' This is particularly true of large urban parishes where the sacramental life of the parish frequently reaches proportions that become exceedingly burdensome for a priest to carry 'gracefully.' " Chicago Studies, November 1983, p. 278

- What would you say to a priest you knew well who had that fear?

PART 4
TOMORROW

So far we have been looking at the contemporary scene in the light of the New Testament and our growing experience.

In both, do we not find a way of life that is true, profound, relevant and free? Is there, anywhere in the world, anything more illuminating and ennobling than the New Testament story when it is allowed to shine in actual people's lives?

Up to now, we have not focused much on the obstacles to this happening. In a movement that is so new, of course there are major difficulties. But it would be sad to let them hide from us the wealth that is already ours.

Even so, it often became obvious that the kind of progress we are learning to look for can only go so far. Yes, two million people in the United States will soon have had a prolonged experience of Christian community, but for the most part that lasts for under three years, and most parishes are unaffected. Yes, a high proportion of Catholics are taking up responsibilities in the Church, but so far the Vatican Council's "definition" of the purpose of the Church as being a "light" to the people influences their involvement very slenderly.

As any car driver knows, the difference between a four cylinder car running on three cylinders, and one running on four, is rather extensive. The feeling is very wide indeed in the Catholic Church today that at the moment we're on three cylinders at most.

However great the present obstacles, there is a confidence that we'll get there in the end. What Catholics, at all levels, are doing now is to consider what developments are needed. Very significant new avenues are being opened up that could greatly enrich the lives of all of us. In the last part of this book, the aim is to reflect, quite concretely, on some of these.

Central to all of them is our ability to have the spiritual enrichment and stimulus of genuine community. How far is that accessible to us? How far will it be accessible in the near future? What steps perhaps need to be taken to make it more accessible, and how urgent are they?

Chapter 1
Communities

ADDITIONAL WAYS OF RECRUITING PASTORS

For the great majority of Catholics today, the parish is their only opportunity of experiencing Christian community. How great, in present circumstances, is that opportunity?

The answer hinges, of course, to a large degree on the pastor. We have already noticed the greatly increased demands on a pastor's time, and that forty percent of them have to serve over twenty-five hundred Catholics. The parishioners are likely to have much higher expectations of true community—from the New Testament, and from their experience of modern life. The average age of priests is now at least fifty-four, and most were trained when liturgy went largely by rote and when a sharing style of leadership was exceptional. Given all these factors it would not be surprising if even the best pastors are unable to create an adequate level of community in such large parishes. *So do we need to find additional ways of recruiting pastors?*

There's also now a responsibility for the future. In terms of Church development, the year 2000 is not long away.

Already, 1,051 of America's 19,244 parishes are without resident priests. Even in the next few years, the number of priestless parishes is expected to increase rapidly.

We are Christians because we belong to the people of God, and therefore we care about the wider Church. There the situation is even more critical. Nearly half the Church's "pastoral centers" (on average 2,214 Catholics) have no resident priest.

Bombarded as we are with so many figures, we have to be careful to weigh the human situation these figures point to. If just a small part of the human story of spiritual deprivation were shown on our TV screens, our reactions might be very strong. An English priest friend of mine visited, in 1980, some dioceses in the Philippines and Peru. One diocese in the Philippines had sixteen priests for one hundred and seventy thousand Catholics, and another had twenty for two hundred and fifty thousand. Many of these could be reached only by horse or by foot—imagine that in the monsoon period! These are typical, *not* the worst, examples. In one town in Peru, there are five priests for a quarter of a million Catholics.

Certainly the dearth of pastors has its advantages. It has helped to channel the work of the full-time ministers into developing the gifts and responsibilities of local people. But as these mature, they particularly need the focal point that only a pastor can usually fully provide, and they need the Eucharist. "As far as I can see," wrote my friend after his journey, "what those communities need is the recognition or authorization that one from their midst (man or woman, married or single) can preside at their Eucharist."[1]

This has been a common view in the Catholic Church since the early 1970's. But is it acceptable? Our view is likely to depend on the importance we attach to smaller Christian communities being a real option for most Americans and to the celibacy of priests as compulsory for them. What is being said on these issues?

Reflection

Before turning to those two issues, you may like to reflect on the increasing dearth of priests.

- What do you think are its good and bad implications for the Church?
- Some fear that far too little is being done to cope with this dearth. A priest expressed this vehemently in 1984 at a meeting of priests: "Many of us celebrate five, six Masses on weekends. Emotionally, we're running out of steam, and my concern is that nobody is really asking the right questions here. Eventually, we will be without the Eucharist."[2]
- Is this too extreme? What is being done in your area, and in the wider Church? What more could be done?

SHOULD CHRISTIAN COMMUNITIES BE SMALLER?

We've seen that the reason why Catholics believe that we should find additional ways to recruit pastors isn't simply that already many parishes are priestless, but because most parishes are already much too big and must before long, with the decreasing number of American priests, get much bigger. The problem isn't that priests aren't able to manage bigger organizations; the difficulty about the size is that it is increasingly preventing Catholics from experiencing Christian community.

It's not much good telling Catholics that we can experience Christ in one another if there isn't much opportunity for most of us to relate to our fellow Christians regularly and deeply. Christianity *does* involve a set of beliefs and values. But these work for us—they enter into our bloodstream—only through our relationships with others.

That is what a Christian community is for. Gradually we come to know these people. We come to know their circumstances, strengths and problems. Looking at others in a spirit of prayer, we see Christ being formed in them, and we even find ourselves contributing to that fruitfulness. As we share our experiences, our prayer, our help and encouragement, we find Christ as the bond that unites us, the life that we share.

If we stay with this process, it makes great demands on us. Yes, we can experience understanding, discernment and encouragement. But the price we pay is our faithfulness and patience.

New strengths are brought out in us. If the group is really Christian it will avoid being self-centered and will reach out to others. Together we share the experience of Christian service.

This kind of Christian community can grow into something strong and stable. The members aren't just joining together for one particular activity, like singing, though a common activity may well set off the whole process. Their community life affects the *whole* of their lives. It gives meaning to their family life, their work, and their goals.

This is how Cardinal Basil Hume of Westminster has described the need for such communities: ''Small groups and basic communities are vital for personal and spiritual formation . . . [They] should be rooted in prayer and shaped by prayer, and the supreme prayer of any group, any community must be the Mass.''[3]

The cardinal does not say that such groups need a priest of their own from one of their own members. But does such a need follow from all we have been seeing?

One reason why it is thought that such groups should be able to have a priest of their own is the fact that the Eucharist should arise out of the center of our Christian lives: the relationships and experiences in which together we are finding Christ. It is *these*, above all, that we want to reflect on and celebrate in a Eucharist. It is simply because a community and its worship are so integrally related that it is natural that the leader of one is the leader of the other.

The other reason is that any close-knit group has a tendency to become self-centered and perhaps disdainful of others. A Christian group that yields to such a tendency is greatly weakened. Our vocation and our strength is to be the people of God, not a loose collection of groups, however worthy.

The role of an *ordained* leader is to consolidate that link with the main body. And the group itself would express that link in many ways, especially by taking part, quite regularly, in parish worship.

The main body, for these small, semi-independent groups, would be the parish. The parish would become "a communion of communities." Most parishes would probably be led by a celibate priest—a married priest might well find running a large parish damaging to married life. But the priest of a small community would be the member most suitable to lead it, married or otherwise.

Perhaps we have so long been accustomed to our present structures, that our parishes becoming "a community of communities" seems a strange or even daunting prospect. So, in the early 1960's, did the prospect of the Mass being said in English.

Just as *today* we can hardly believe that the Mass was for centuries said in a language that very few could understand, will we *tomorrow* see these small, semi-independent communities such an obvious consequence of all we've come to believe, and such a natural and fruitful part of most parishes, that we shall find it difficult to understand why it took so long to recognize their necessity?

This kind of parish cannot arise overnight. Training, organization, and suitable ways of introducing them must be arranged. Do the statistics suggest that we have time on our side?

Reflection

"Parish leaders now realize that people need small, intimate experience of community if they are to feel themselves part of the parish" (Thomas Sweetser, Successful Parishes, p. 177).

- Do you, and the people you know, have this need? If so, to what extent is it being met at present?

"I would argue strongly from within my own experience that the parish can be given new life if it is regarded and organized as a community of communities, as a resource center and a focus for the coordination of pastoral and missionary activities" (Cardinal Hume, archbishop of Westminster, 1985).

- What would be lost, and what would be gained, by our larger parishes becoming a communion of communities?
- How would you envisage such communities operating if they are desirable (e.g., number of members; essential and possible activities; frequency of meetings)?
- If it is appropriate to ordain married people (to be considered in our next section), the leaders of many of these small groups might be priests. Leaving the matter of compulsory celibacy for our next section, what advantages and disadvantages might there eventually be in that happening in your parish?

SHOULD MARRIED PEOPLE BE ORDAINED AS PRIESTS?

Many of the people who think that suitable married people should be ordained as priests stress that if this is to be done, it should be done for the right reasons. Obviously the increasingly grave shortage of priests is an important factor. But such a profound change from our present custom should be seen to arise from *theological principles*, not from panic about numbers.

Only recently has it been possible for the Church as a whole to seriously discuss this question, because we are only now emerging from centuries of depreciation of human sexuality and of seeing priesthood as primarily to do with a supranatural kind of life, untainted by the secular life.

Obviously a person whose role is to lead a community in

"the whole work of bringing salvation to people in the material and social dimension in which they actually live" must be closely involved in the secular life of the people around that community. A pastor of a parish is increasingly expected to be part of the family of the parish community and integrated into its lifestyle. In the smaller communities that are being envisaged, that would of course be even more so.

Therefore on the theological level, Catholics are discussing whether *some* parish priests should be married people, and, as we have just seen, whether many of the smaller communities that should be developed would not have a most urgent pastoral need for their leaders to be priests (mainly married), so as to give them stability and a firm identity. Our more developed understanding of Christian leadership and Christian community would seem to make having some married priests both enriching and necessary.

No one is denying that celibacy both has been and is, in many priests, an inspiring sign of his special love of Christ and dedication to him, and his firm hope in the future God has promised. Unfortunately, it can make priests appear to be a separate and superior class, however much they themselves may regret that.

The positive values of celibacy are too strong to be abandoned as an important vocation in those called to it. What is being questioned very widely indeed is whether it should be *compulsory* for priests. Will celibacy hinder the work of some priests today and tomorrow? Will it make it more difficult for them to be closely involved with the people around, especially with their learning to deepen their own life of love with the help of their sexuality? And, perhaps above all, *should this high Christian ideal be enforced by law?*

When we turn from the theological side of the question to the matter of numbers, we are certainly not leaving the question of spiritual need. Many bishops have stressed this. "I foresee the ordaining to the priesthood of married men in certain parts of the world as the only way to bring the sacraments of Eucharist and reconciliation to people" (Cardinal Hume). "If the Eucharist is to be the center of our lives, we must ordain married men. It is as simple as that" (the archbishop of Semarang).

But *would Catholics accept married priests?* This question was put to the delegates to the National Pastoral Congress in England and Wales in 1980. Two thirds of the lay delegates and nearly four fifths of the priest delegates would accept married priests and over one third of all delegates would accept women priests.[4] In America, in 1983, fifty-eight percent of U.S. Catholics favored married priests, and the strongest support was from 18–29 year olds.[5]

Another important factor is how *Catholics perceive celibacy as a compulsory element in a vocation to the priesthood.* A 1983 survey of Catholic vocations in the United States showed that young people are *not* less religious than those of twenty years ago. Indeed, a Gallup poll in 1980 found that seven percent of American Catholics over the age of eighteen would be interested in either the full-time ministry or in some other religious work as a career.

But when it comes to priesthood, celibacy is seen as a principal problem because of "new attitudes about sexuality, personal freedoms and ways of living."[6] Similar conclusions were drawn in Britain in the same year by a group set up by the bishops of England and Wales. It found that even good Catholic parents rarely considered the possibility of a vocation to the priesthood for their sons, and that celibacy was among the obstacles. An English Catholic sociologist was able to add, from his own 1978 national survey, that it is *among the young* that a celibate life (priest or sister) is least favored. As many as forty-seven percent of 15-24 year olds would be displeased if one of their children were seriously thinking of being a priest or sister (of those over 65, only nine percent would be displeased). His view is that "Catholics are at least intuitively aware of the value of celibacy as a freely given offering with love to God and the Christian community. But increasingly they see no value, but only a distorting irrelevance in the unwarranted identification of celibacy with priesthood."[7]

Obviously the three questions we have been considering are closely related:

1. Should we consider additional ways of recruiting priests?
2. Should the experience of semi-independent smaller communities be made widely available?
3. Should married people be ordained as priests?

If the Church were to say "yes" to all three, then we have some urgent work ahead of us. But do we need to be too worried? A high proportion of all sectors of the Church would accept it, and the approval of the New Testament writers would be unanimous, as we recover the values they considered so important.

Reflection

"Since we affirm the centrality of the Eucharist, we must consider, and urgently, how best to call forth from the community sufficient candidates for the priesthood. We shall soon arrive at the situation (if we have not in many places already reached it) when bishops will have to select from within the local community persons of appropriate experience, age and integrity to be ordained to the priesthood. They may, indeed, be married men" (Cardinal Basil Hume, June 1985).

- Do you consider this a sufficient reason for ordaining married people? Are there other good reasons?
- "Celibacy proclaims that there is a greater intimacy than the intimacy of marriage" (Abbot Thomas Keating, 1981).[8]
- "Cannot Christian marriage help lead the priest to that human maturity and capability of love which will enable the priest to make God's love visible to others?"[9]
- We are all aware of arguments for and against compulsory cel-

ibacy for priests. Which of the arguments you have considered seem most decisive to you? Do they apply equally to pastors of parishes and to leaders of small but stable groups, if we have them in the future?

- How important is this matter for the life of the Church today?

Chapter 2
Becoming "A Light to All People"

HOW LONG A SLEEP?

None of us would want to come to a firm view about any group until we had decided what it was for. Is it to make money, to provide sporting facilities, to have sneakers prohibited from all public places, or to confront the neighborhood with art? With regard to the Church, the New Testament makes its purpose perfectly clear: it is to help bring about God's reign. But what does that mean in practice in a modern industrialized society?

This question is as new as the ones about local Christian communities. For centuries, historical circumstances led the Church to turn in on itself. Deep-seated assumptions naturally need time to change. Today we're just at the beginning of what should be the most fruitful discovery in the whole of the twentieth century. God's rule—that process of creative, loving transformation—isn't simply for us: it's for everyone!

As we begin to appreciate that the job of Christians is to tell this news, of course we ask questions. How do you actually do that in our modern world? And, more concretely, what is already being done?

First, what is being done? How far have we got in this new development?

An outsider reading recent papal teaching might well conclude that most Catholics, by now, must have made this job of "evangelization" (the Latin for good-news-giving) their priority. When John Paul I reminded the entire Church that "its first duty is that of evangelization," he was only expressing what Paul VI had most strongly underlined. But, seven years later, Alvin Illig, the director of the National Catholic Evangelization Association, believed that only three percent of American Catholics see that as a priority. And the number of converts, relative to the number of Catholics, is much less than half of what it was in 1960.

In a moment we shall see that this is the beginning, not the end, of the story. But the rest will make more sense if we focus for a moment on the first chapter. What is this figure of three percent, from a nationally recognized expert, saying to us?

Is it saying that a Church that claims to have been given the truth about human life hasn't yet sorted out what it should do about that?

Is it saying that America as a whole, where forty percent are unchurched, is not being given from most Catholics the light it needs?

George Gallup called the Catholic Church in America "the sleeping giant of evangelization." You have the heritage, he said; you have the people; and you have the structures. But you don't have the fire.

What is Christianity good for without fire?

Your answers to those questions will probably be your assessment of where we have to go so far in our story. If our story is to have a happy ending, we need to face up to assessing our present progress, whatever be the painfulness. But a second chapter in the story is beginning to unfold. The giant's slumbers could be temporary!

CLEVELAND, A PIONEER

Cleveland, Ohio has long been a target for American satire ("Pittsburgh without the glitter" happens to be my favorite). Friends who live there make a point of showing me its more elegant parts. But however you assess that city's claims to beauty, it is acknowledged to be one of the leaders in evangelization. Many parts of America are still at the first chapter stage. But in Cleveland they began to move on more from there in 1980. What happens when you do that? What are the difficulties that are at present blocking progress in most places? How do you begin to overcome them?

Note the date when Cleveland began to tackle these questions. Until 1980, hardly any diocese had tried to bring evangelization to the forefront of its agenda. Yes, Paul VI had strongly asked *all* Catholics to do that in 1975, and in 1976 the American bishops had dutifully made a statement that evangelization is a major priority. But apart from setting up an excellent office in Washington, under Alvin Illig, not a great deal was done.

It was only in 1982 that it looked as though the tide might be turning. The need for that was acknowledged at the meeting of U.S. bishops. The archbishop of Santa Fe told the bishops that when Paul VI asked that evangelization should come first, "it was looked upon by many priests and bishops simply as another church program." Few were able to see in the Pope's document "a carefully structured outline and the potential for unifying all our pastoral activities. Today the Spirit is guiding us to rediscover the fundamental task of the Church as that of evangelization."

So when, two years before that, Cleveland started its campaign, it was among the pioneers in this rediscovery. It has had more experience than most of coping with the problems. We are watching the giant's first stirrings, before the time of full awakening.

EVANGELIZATION IN PRACTICE

To understand what Cleveland and other places are doing to-day, and what we all may do tomorrow, we must briefly recall what actually happens when evangelization takes place. The name may suggest to many people the pushy Jehovah's Witness, a TV evangelist always asking for more money, or a fire and brimstone preacher. But we know that it's in fact a profoundly personal, human thing. It's the people who see Jesus in us and say: "Show us more."

Communication is obviously essential: somehow people have to "see" our Christianity if they're ever going to say that. But, just as obviously, it all hinges on Jesus being in us in such a way as to provoke that response.

Are we a people who have been fired by that Nazareth manifesto to bring good news to the poor and liberty to the captives, not as a notional proposition, but here and now, for the people we can touch? Or are we people who are content to have inherited a private deal with God that will ensure *our* salvation, while other people in their need are ignored as not our business?

The first thing that needs to happen is for the Catholic Church to recover its New Testament heritage. Much of this book has been devoted to describe how this is actually happening. In many places people's gifts are being honored and given scope; deep relationships of love and encouragement are being made more possible; maturity and responsibility are being valued; we are making our own St. Paul's cry: "For freedom Christ has set us free" (Gal 5:1).

Here we already notice how the various aspects of Christian life that we have been exploring throughout this book interlock with one another. Christian life, we have seen, happens when the following come together:

> *The Fire:*   Reflection on the New Testament in the light
>   of our experience, prayer and worship

The Setting:	Community
The Thrust:	Recognition, encouragement and use of gifts
The Direction:	Shared responsibility and leadership

Evangelization isn't some optional extra that we may possibly choose to add to this interlocking whole. *The parts we have listed are simply incomplete without it.* Of what use are reflection on the New Testament, prayer and worship if they have not really fired us with enthusiasm and love to give to others what we ourselves have found? Of what use is our recognizing our gifts if we don't value them as a means to bring Christ to others?

Part of the difficulty we at present have is, of course, that neither "the others," nor communicating our Christian life to them, is very much the experience of most of us. Just as kissing is merely a notion until you see someone you love, so evangelization is just a long, ambiguous Latin word until you meet someone with whom you want to share the good news. Somehow those "others," in their need for Christ, have first to become real for us.

DIFFERENT PLACES, DIFFERENT WAYS

One of the best ways of moving toward this, Cleveland has found, is to have a group in the parish that discerns this as a fundamental need and helps open the eyes of the parish to that.

An early step might be to make sure the parish has a welcoming committee. Their job is to make it known in the neighborhood that all are really welcome and to ensure that anyone who comes is made to feel at home. Already the atmosphere and the outlook of the parish can be changing!

That might be followed up by a census. You might divide the parish into, say, six regions, with one person taking responsibility for each. They find twelve volunteers for each region to help to take the census.

The purpose is to make a genuinely human outreach to everyone in the parish. You're not going to their homes to bombard them with Christian doctrines but to say: "Here we are. Can we help in any way? We're trying to be a better Christian group in this neighborhood; and we'd sincerely value your suggestions."

If this is done in the right spirit, this is a moving experience for those taking part in it. Of course there are slammed doors and cold disdain. Evangelization has never been an easy option. But there is also the surprised delight in some that a Church has reached out in this way: we know that forty percent of inactive Catholics have thought of coming back and could appreciate an invitation (Gallup). Those taking part in the census feel themselves the trusted ambassadors of their parish and they experience at first hand, often in simple quiet ways, that this speaks deeply to some people. The parish itself can feel that it's now on the move.

As it becomes known in the neighborhood that the Christian community really cares about others, offers a warm welcome, and listens as well as speaks, other ways of reaching out to others seem to arise naturally. Cleveland told me of thirty-three they know to have been used with success in their parishes.

Often the culmination of these approaches is a program called RCIA (Rite of the Christian Initiation of Adults) where the parishioners invite interested non-Catholics to come along with their inquiries. As sponsors or catechists some are in direct, regular contact with potential converts in their journey toward faith, and the whole parish should join in celebrating the stages on the way. We old-time Catholics become aware that *we too* are on a journey. Our complacency diminishes; like St. Paul we "keep striving" (Phil 3:12). And a key part of our annual experience is converts we know discovering what Christianity means to them, as we follow them on their journey.

There are innumerable strong testimonies, throughout the world, to how the lives of individuals and whole parishes have been deeply transformed through this RCIA process. For the Catholics who consent to be closely involved, as well as the converts, it is often a conversion experience.

This process can be used just as fruitfully to help Catholics in whom the faith has never really taken root. In 1981 the diocese of Stockton, California began to work on the assumption that "none of the kids have been evangelized." The bishop himself testified to the outcome. "It is just unbelievable," he said. "For the first time our young people have an experience of faith."[1]

That was no pious dream. When they had finished the two year RCIA process, many of these 16-18 year olds committed themselves to turning up each month for two years to be sponsors for the next "wave" of young people. I've never visited Stockton, but it must be the kind of diocese where young people feel at home. Just look at what they want their parish liturgy committees to do: "to promote *joy* and prayer." St. Paul would indeed have approved of that combination.

Reflection

- Have you had experience of adults being helped to see the truth of Christianity? If so, what did it tell you about how this can happen?
- What do your non-Catholic friends know about the Catholic faith and way of life? What opportunities do they have of knowing more?
- What is your parish already doing to help the parishioners to reach out to others? Should it do more? Who would do it?

- How many of us could benefit from a "refresher" like those young people in Stockton?

"An awful lot of proclamation of the good news goes on through the helping relationship" (Patrick Brennan, Evangelization Office, Chicago).[2]

- Do you agree?

"Evangelization loses much of its force if it does not take into account the people to whom it is concretely addressed, if it does not use their language, their signs and symbols, if it does not answer the questions they are themselves asking, if it does not touch and move their concrete life" (Pope Paul VI).[3]

- How can we better take into account the people to whom we try to address the good news?

Chapter 3
Christianity in the Marketplace

What happens in a parish when Christianity comes out of the closet into the market-place?

The whole movement we've been following in this book leads to that question. Christianity in the marketplace is what community, gifts, prayer, parish councils and pastors are for, and what evangelization very largely consists of. If a local church isn't in practice about "restoring sight to the blind and liberating captives," it can't, according to the New Testament, claim to be in the business of evangelization. It has simply not found what John Paul II called its "distinctive vocation and its deepest identity." If my local church doesn't help me appreciate the importance of *all* the main aspects of my life—my *work*, my *living in this neighborhood* and *in this country*, as well as the ones we've seen—then it's not helping me be a complete Christian person who is able to show Christ very convincingly to others.

MY WORK

For most of our waking hours the majority of us are working. What importance has our Christianity for this large portion of our lives?

It has some importance, certainly. We feel called to be honest in business dealings, to give our employer a good day's work for our pay, and to be friendly with the people with whom we work.

But a full kind of Christian life isn't just about not cheating employers and being a friendly kind of person. It's about ordinary people like us being partners in God's transformation of the world. And it's about our being God's partners, not just in "churchy" things but in our whole lives, most of which we spend working.

But is it realistic to think of my job as being something so grand as that kind of partnership with God? It might be easier if my work consisted of making beautiful things. An artist is aware of creative powers and of using them as a contribution, perhaps, to something significant. But a cab driver? An attorney?

The more we think of ourselves and the people we know, the more we realize that there are no easy answers to this question. It's not just that many people have repetitive, mechanical jobs, like operating the same piece of machinery in the same way endlessly. Those who work in a big corporation can have a similar feeling. You may have no direct contact with the product or its quality or its usefulness to people. It may seem impossible to have any influence on the conditions of work. Your work seems to consist of just clocking in each day and being no more than a cog in a big machine. Christianity *may* be about making us more human so as to join in the transformation of human life. But certainly not in my work. Not in what I do in most of my waking hours!

So for a question that concerns so much of most of our lives, there are no easy answers.

Every person's situation is different. I may need to ask myself such questions as: Have I really explored what my gifts are? Do I sufficiently appreciate and use my gifts as talents given me by a loving and gracious God so that I may join in his work of serving people? Why did I choose my present job: because it was the only one available, or simply for my own career purposes, or also with a wish to help people? What influence *could* I have in my workplace to make its conditions more human and its product of better human usefulness?

These are all questions about Christian ministry. Through the way we react to them we can do far more central Christian service than many purely ''churchy'' ministries.

The answers may be vital—but certainly not uniform or easy. Each of us needs some help with them. Which of us does not need people to help us recognize our gifts and assist our choices and opportunities? We need support and encouragement as we enter this largely unchartered field. Isn't it here, above all, that the Church will be of help?

IS THE CHURCH HELPING YOU?

As we consider that last question, we can start by hearing how a sales manager answered it in 1976:

> I am now a sales manager of a major steel company. In the almost thirty years of my professional career, my church has never once suggested that there be any type of accounting of my on-the-job ministry to others. My church has never once offered to improve those skills which could make me a better minister, nor has it ever asked if I needed any kind of support in what I was doing.
>
> There was never an inquiry into the types of ethical decisions I must face, or whether I seek to communicate the faith to my co-workers. I have never been in a congregation where there was any type of public affirmation of a ministry in my career. In short, I must conclude that my church really doesn't have the least interest whether or how I minister in my daily work. [1]

Catholic church leaders are aware of the force of that anguished complaint. In 1981, the archbishop of St. Louis acknowledged that. He read that sales manager's statement to a large meeting in his diocese and then made this confession:

Those words draw attention to a blindspot in Catholic thinking. For this blindspot people like myself—bishops and
priests—bear considerable responsibility.

No wonder the reports in 1980 from the dioceses in England
for the National Pastoral Congress showed that ''there is little or
no appreciation among the people of any real relation between
their faith and the work they do. All consider that there ought to
be, and that the Church needs to help people to realize how Christian beliefs are related to work.''[2]

Part of the American Church is beginning to give that help.
Of course most of the help we need cannot come from general
statements or sermons—though we may have a need for those
also. Our primary need is to share experiences, understanding and
encouragement with people who face similar situations to ours.

In a spirit of prayer, we help each other to appreciate our gifts
and what we may be being called to do with them. We come to
recognize opportunities of humanizing the conditions of our work,
perhaps in the ways that major decisions are made. Renew and
other programs are providing at least some encouragement to our
coming together in this way. Whether they are doing so sufficiently in your area, only you can say.

Groups of Christians who regularly meet to tackle such problems are the spearhead of the Church. They show the world its
human, transforming face. They show that Christ cares.

OUR WHOLE ENVIRONMENT

Of course work isn't the only aspect of our everyday human
life where that is necessary.

In a very large Benedictine house I know, two unobtrusive

members quietly, but persistently, changed the atmosphere over the years, so that now it's far more a home than an institution. So, in many neighborhoods, a minority can, if they really want to, gradually affect what "goes" and what is not accepted, at least in some areas.

As Christians, we have a "vision" of warm, unselfish, patient love (1 Cor 13), of the elimination of human inequalities (the Beatitudes), of the unity of the human race (Gal 3:28), and of a transformed future for the whole of creation when God's reign comes in all its fullness (Rom 8:21). And what we as Christians are "about" is incarnation: giving legs to these ideals through a realistic response to the actual human situation.

Could not several outward-looking groups in a neighborhood lead an increasing number of people to show respect and some concern for one another and become more aware of who is suffering injustice and hardship?

It won't be an easy ride. If we really care about injustice, we'll be asking for work to be done to sort out the facts and to see how they might be coped with. We'll be liable to upset vested interests in business and politics.

We'll have to try to do that in a *Christian* way. Through prayer, we'll keep to our vision, our hope and our love. We'll avoid a merely negative approach and care even more for the long-term, positive transformation of our neighborhood—and our world.

This, after all, is the good news we have been called to proclaim to the world: God is love, and *therefore* he is transforming all of human destiny.

Proclaiming the Gospel consists in showing that this transformation both can happen and is happening in human history. We're *not* telling people that it's happening only in us Christians. We're saying that love is the only thing that really "works," because the deepest reality of all is love, and that the destiny of *all* people is to be that person's children. *"Anyone* who loves is a child of God'' (1 Jn 4:7). Christians are simply the sign, the beachhead, of what is help to be offered to every human being.

So we're not telling people what they don't already know at some level of their thinking and feeling. We've all met many non-Christians who try to be loving and responsible, sometimes heroically, in spite of no obvious help from religion.

The evangelization they will listen to isn't a set of doctrines or of religious practices by themselves. They need to see a body of people who are boldly and creatively open to modern life and whose beliefs and practices help them to make sense of life both in themselves and in others. They want Christianity to show them what life actually looks like in people who back fully the kind of beliefs that they themselves can't be sure of: in the world's future, say, and in the ultimate validity of love.

"Does your Christianity shut you into an aloof or selfish system?" they are asking us. "Or does it lead you into tackling courageously, out of love for people, the problems and opportunities of our neighborhood and our world? Is there a warmth, a joy, and a celebration about your work there that finds expression in your worship? Do you in practice recognize the dedication, wisdom, skills and achievements of non-Christians so that you can join us, or are you more interested in the prestige of your own system?"

When we think of that implicit invitation and of how recent developments in our Church have made it possible for us to hear it and accept it, we may feel that we stand at a major crossroads in our history.

But how can we, in practice, take up that invitation?

Many individuals already have. So have religious orders who take a deliberate choice to work as Christian communities affirming and helping the humane work of others.

By 1980, very little had been done to help most individuals or communities to move in that direction:

There is, at present, no sustained pastoral mobilization of lay energies toward world transformation, no compelling sense of the world of work as, genuinely, a *religious* vocation, no appropriate vision with powerful leverage to criticize the imperfections and rank injustices of the social order. The absence of these creates a situation of pastoral tragedy and represents a serious dereliction of duty on the part of the Church. For their absence means the effective abdication of the Church's vocation to transform the world (John A. Coleman S.J.).[3]

In 1985, there were still only two percent of committed Catholics who had climbed out of the closet into the marketplace, so far as parish activities were concerned. Renew should be beginning to open out those wider horizons for the people it has touched. But no program can do much more than help with the initial boost. The long-term momentum can come only from our own experience of turning our eyes to the people around us with Jesus' love, repect, and compassion.

For many of us, the best chance of our being able to have such experience may be the kind of local church that Dolores Leckey has for many years been gently putting before us.

It is a small ecumenical Protestant church in Washington D.C., called Church of the Savior. All who want to join it have to make two commitments. They have to promise to try to discover their true self and God, and they also have to promise to care for some segment of human needs, either alone or with others.

This is the pattern we've already seen: a church operating by the belief that everyone is gifted. Its purpose is to help its members discover their gifts and to use them in some kind of service, either in some formal ministry, or in more individual, spontaneous action.

The kind of initiatives this church has taken up is the kind you might expect from such a body. There is a home for dependent children, which tries to befriend the real parents and facilitate healing and reconciliation. There is a low-key Christian coffee house, art and bookstore, where the volunteer staff offer conversation to those who want it, but who would never cross the threshold of a ''normal'' church.

The archbishop of Baltimore called the Church ''a living sign of God's concern for mankind: a sign of hope and promise for the world.'' Christians who lived as members of a community like the Church of the Savior in Washington might have *the context* they need for being that.

Reflection

We are looking at the Church of the Savior in Washington to see how our own local church could better fulfill its vocation of being what the archbishop of Baltimore described. Here are just a few of the questions that Washington church may raise for us:

- How far can a local church be for the people around it ''a living sign of God's concern for mankind'' if its policy is mainly shaped by people whose gaze (understandably) is turned inward into the parish structures and the maintenance of the parish plant, rather than to the world around them?
- Is the main policy of my local church turned outward? If so, how did that happen? If not, what, realistically, could be done about that?
- I know few Catholics who would advocate abandoning the parish structure. But do parishes need within them some communities of a hundred or two like the Church of the Savior? If so, which of its characteristics might eventually be valuable in your parish? If it were desirable, how could such communities be started in your parish, either now or later?

Chapter 4
Sharing Responsibility

What kind of leadership will we need in the parishes and small communities through which the Church can in fact be a sign of God's concern for all men and women?

Here again our reflections may be more realistic and practicable if we start with what has been happening for several years in the Church of Christ the Savior. Here is Dolores Leckey's description: "The pastor, Gordon Cosby, has a role that is very well defined. He consciously evokes the gifts of the community. He tests people's felt call to ministry. He ministers to the ministers. He provides spiritual direction to those who seek him. He leads the weekly worship, giving great care and attention to this central act of the community. He prays and is known as a man of prayer. He leads retreats. He coordinates many of the missions. He is about the business of 'giving it all away,' and enabling others to function."

In brief, he is the leader of an orchestra, not a one-man band.

And Leckey asks whether we can't learn something from that. She believes we need communities where "all the people can exercise responsibility for prayer and worship, for spiritual development, for the needs of society—when ministry is shared. The existential power of the Church as Christ made visible is diminished, I think, when we categorically assign prayer and worship to one group (the ordained and the vowed) and picket lines to others (the laity). But the face of Christ is resplendently present

93

when all the members participate in the ministry each according to his/her charism and call.''[1]

HELP FROM THE NEW TESTAMENT

One of the main ways in which the power of our Church gets diminished is our dividing up the Church into clergy and laity.

The clergy are the officers. You can't become an officer unless you are celibate. The laity are the ''other ranks.''

Where this mentality persists, there is no chance of the kind of leadership or local community we have been describing. But a better knowledge of the New Testament is gradually rescuing us from this restriction.

In the New Testament, we saw, there were *no* ''other ranks.'' No one was a layman or laywoman, in the sense of being on the fringe of a field of action or a topic. In another sense it relates to the New Testament description of the Church as ''the people of God.'' But to that *every* Christian equally belonged. Indeed, everyone had a gift. The less impressive gifts were just as indispensable as the more impressive ones. Responsibility for the community's life and activity was shared by everyone. There were indeed leaders: but, like Gordon Cosby, the leaders' business was one of ''giving it all away,'' of enabling others to function. He or she was more like the chairperson of a department than a head teacher over young pupils.

Ministry as Jesus had founded it—Christians sharing in God's whole work of loving service to the human race—was much too strong and wide a force to be limited to one type. The situation *we* inherit is of a long period of history where there was a strong tendency for it to be limited to priesthood. But, in New Testament times, ministry took effect in the wide and shared range of activities we saw earlier, like prophecy, teaching, healing, consoling, encouraging, spreading the word, serving the poor, and a host of others. Any ministry was open to *anyone* who had that particular gift. You didn't have to be celibate—though celibacy was valued if you were called to it.

No one was particularly concerned with tabulating this force into tidy categories or titles. If you spoke out about what the good news was saying to a group of Christians here and now, then you were known to be a prophet; if you served others, particularly the poor, then you might be called a deacon (Greek for servant); if you were the leader, or one of the *body* of leaders (leadership was often corporate), then a leadership-type name was eventually chosen from the language of your country. In a Greek-type of community you might be known as an "overseer" (bishop), or, in a Jewish-type of community, a "presbyter." In some communities prophets and teachers were leaders, and they didn't start to be called bishop or presbyter until later. But the focus of interest was on the giftedness and the responsiblities *of the whole community*, not on the leadership. The job of the leader, as Paul loved to emphasize, was simply "to build you up."

All this activity, as we've seen, was *primarily* to advance God's reign in the world. Only gradually did the ministries of bishop and presbyter focus primarily on worship, absorb most of the other ministries, and entail a different life-style.

All that came later. It was a question of gradual limitations being caused by the circumstances of different places and times. Most of them had positive sides to them and fitted well the period in which they arose.

TODAY

The new thing today is that we are able to overcome many of those limitations. We are beginning to regain the vitality and

the relevance of the New Testament age. We could add to them
the advantages of our own age, when science offers an unparal-
leled opportunity to transform our work economically, politically
and socially.

What will the Church look like as we do that?

Of course, there'd still be the Pope, the bishops and the
priests. But in a local church, as we have seen, there could be
several priests. There would be the pastor of the parish, and some
of the leaders of the smaller communities.

The bishops and priests would, of course, be *ordained* to
their ministries. The Church would continue to affirm their gift of
leadership and commission them to exercise it for this locality.
But the Church would do the same for a range of other ministries.
It might be the people who run the parish's shelter for the home-
less, who are concerned on our behalf with confronting injustice
in the neighborhood, who coordinate religious education, who
preach, who teach the faith to converts. Might each area choose
the ministries it will affirm publicly by ordination according to its
own specific needs? Might a policy of this kind make much clearer
to Catholics and to others the rich variety of the power to serve
people that Christ has given *this* community. Would the power of
"the Church as Christ made visible" be more evident and ap-
pealing? And would it rescue the pastor from being expected to
have *all* the skills, when everyone knows that to be an absurd ex-
pectation?

Every parent, of course, knows the danger of giving special
encouragement to *one* of several children. Some of the others can
feel overlooked. Today the new stress in some churches on married men becoming deacons has often led to a widespread impres-
sion that to work for the Church in any substantial capacity you
must be ordained. When that happens, the informal ministries we
saw to be so important are undervalued. There could be less danger of this when we make a fuller use of the power of ministry that
Christ gave us and expand the present three types of ordained lead-

ership. Even so, like wise parents, we would need to bear in mind the danger, and to make sure that recognizing and encouraging the informal ministries is just as integral to the life of any local community.

Reflection

- At present, only bishops, priests and deacons are ordained; and yet in many parishes there are other "professional" ministers, like directors of religious education, counselors, youth workers and others. Do you think that some of these should be ordained? If so, what do you think would be gained? How could we ensure that the pastor is still the foremost leader?
- How, in today's and tomorrow's parish, can we best support and encourage part-time ministries?

"Few parishes recognize anyone for extraordinary service as a parent, shopkeeper, laborer, civil servant, or professional" (Thomas Sweetser, Successful Parishes, p. 147).

- Do you think they should? If so, how?
- Do you think we need "one or more full-time professional ministers who will help surface, train, and bring to the attention of the total community the large array of unnoticed, gifted people in their midst, rather than they themselves perform or organize all the services of the community" (Dennis Geaney, Emerging Ministries, p.108)?

"The clergy/laity division was to a large extent a deviation from the authentic ideal of Christian community, and no theological justification can be found for allowing it to continue. . . . (We must not equate) designated (ordained) ministry with either 'superior status' or 'ruling.' . . . The division does stand as one of the major barriers to formation of a Christian community in which all have basic equality and dignity as brothers and sisters in Christ" (Bernard Cooke, Ministry to Word and Sacraments, pp. 197, 398).

The clergy/laity division emerged clearly in the fourth century and gradually became stronger until eventually the word "Church" was taken to mean the clergy. No longer was it the chief responsibility of the whole Christian community to bear witness to the Gospel. All active roles in the Church belonged to the clergy. They were the rulers, and the laity were the ruled. And, since the rulers largely distanced themselves from the secular world, so, quite extensively, did Christian activity.

Major factors that caused this division were:

(a) Bishops, priests and deacons became full-time occupations.
(b) They had a different way of life.
(c) Clerical celibacy was understood as a sign that the clergy were holier than the laity and should live separately in a more "sacred" world.

- What causes the division today? How damaging is it? Many pastors and many laity want to dismantle it. How can that be done?

Chapter 5
"Experts in Humanity"

THE HUMAN REALITY IN EACH OTHER

George was driving home from work one winter evening. As he reached the house—near the top of a steep hill—he noticed that his wife's car still had its lights on.

"These women!" George thought complacently. "Bad luck they're incompetent with machines!" And he went into the house to get Jane's keys.

Jane was apologetic. She seemed tacitly to accept that *men* were the people with mechanical know-how. *They* were the practical ones.

George advanced toward Jane's car and was about to unlock its door when he half noticed that something was missing. He looked around. Yes, something *was* missing: his car. He had forgotten to secure the handbreak.

I've known George and Jane well since 1967. They both inherited this stereotype of men as by nature the competent, if not dominant, fixers, and of women as by nature simply the gentle, passive, homemakers. In fact they're too intelligent and too close to one another and their five children to apply that extensively—and George likes to tell that story against himself. Theirs is a relaxed, kindly, affectionate and outward-going family. Their good-humored shedding of that stereotype has had much to do with that.

The Church wishes to be an "expert in humanity," Paul VI told the United Nations. In this book we have been following some of that story. It's a story of getting through to the human reality of others so that we can relate to them fruitfully. And the purpose of this is to *be* truly Church: the beachhead of transformed humanity as a sign of hope to everyone.

So the question that we Christians have chiefly to ask ourselves is: Are we sufficiently becoming that beachhead?

To an extent we are. Many of us are growing with and for others in Christian communities. We are opening ourselves to each other's gifts. We are finding ways of applying them, as a team, in the service of others. Leadership is becoming more shared and enabling. It's sadly true that many have the pain of having access to little of this in their parishes. We owe them real sympathy for their pain.

But this should not block out from our consciousness the widespread advances or prevent our gratitude for so much good.

The story of George and Jane reminds us that overcoming false stereotypes is essential to our becoming that beachhead. How can a non-Christian recognize a transformed humanity in us if we don't relate humanly to men and women, to blacks and whites, to the poor, to foreigners? Many of the advances we have seen *could* leave us just a more friendly, congenial, but inward-looking club. To allow such an outcome would obviously be a betrayal of our Christian vocation.

BLACKS AND HISPANICS

In 1976 a black priest was named auxiliary bishop in Newark, New Jersey, and six years later he described what happened to him. "I had not been here a week when a well-meaning priest took me aside and told me as kindly as he could that I had to be prepared to face the fact that I would not be accepted in every church in the archdiocese and that 'in fact some would reject me; some had already rejected my coming.' "[1]

The parishes where that happened were clearly clubs, not Christian churches. If they had been churches, they would at least have tried to draw into their bloodstream what Paul VI called the "gifts of blackness": the warmth and spontaneity in relationships and in prayer; the *wholeness* of blacks' approach to life, so that feelings and intellect are integrated; the sense of joy; the deep commitment to community as a human value. Any parish can benefit from that kind of infusion. And to the enrichment of *all* their people, many do.

> Hispanics, too, often experience coldness or rejection. "I will share with you now what racism has meant to the Hispanic men, women and children who constitute seventy-five percent of the people I serve. To us:
>
> Racism is seeing ourselves on TV only as drunken bandits, subservient domestics or flamboyant dancers.
>
> Racism is having to prove my citizenship simply because my face is brown.
>
> Racism is being subjected to police brutality, being considered guilty until I can prove I am innocent.
>
> Racism is being tolerated, but never welcomed.
>
> These and countless other experiences cause the Hispanic to live in constant fear. It is the fear of being ignored, of being rejected, of being ridiculed. (The bishop of El Paso, 1981).[2]

Yet the Hispanic appreciation of the person and of the extended family contributes much to the Church when sympathetically encouraged. Has the fact that only a third of Hispanics (nearly twenty million in the United States) attend church services, and the fact that sixty percent of second generation Hispanics in New York can't name any of the seven sacraments, *something* to do with whites' attitudes?

Everyone knows that it is seldom easy to begin integrating a different race into a local community—though, once begun, their human qualities and gifts often generate a strong momentum.

Of course, it is *trying* that counts. But if a local church does not try, it is difficult to see how it can plausibly claim to embody God's promise of human transformation.

SEXISM

How can the Catholic Church cope with the problem of sexism?

Here the stakes are even higher than with racism. First, sexism poisons the wholeness of a person's humanity, because it consists of a woman conniving with the fallacy that she is by nature less rational than a man, and of a man conniving with the fallacy that he is by nature less intuitive and caring than a woman. Unfortunately, a great deal in the Christian tradition encourages sexism.

The other reason why much can be lost arises from the fact that we pride ourselves on considerable progress toward the liberation of women. We are hardly likely to believe that the Church stands for human transformation if it is weak in this field.

The problem is critical and urgent. But there is no chance of our solving it unless we face up to the facts.

STRONG FEELINGS

One is very obvious: the strong, and contradictory, emotions involved.

If anyone still believes that only "way out" *women* feel deeply affronted by sexist Church attitudes and practices, that person should talk with women in responsible positions in parishes or dioceses about their feelings. It is a moving and humbling experience. That kind of experience helped the Canadian bishops to say in 1983: "Let us recognize the ravages of sexism and our own male appropriation of Church institutions and numerous aspects of the Christian life."

Women can feel oppressed, if not embittered, but *men* can feel that the only world they're psychologically at home with is profoundly threatened. Society expects them to be the one in command and to leave domesticity—if not tenderness—to the woman. People believe *in their minds* that women should be equal. But few have seriously considered what that implies for people's inner and social lives.

In specifically Church-related activities, change can also feel deeply repugnant to men. For many centuries, active participation in worship has been the prerogative of males—though the fact that eighty percent of American Catholics have at least come to terms with women's increased involvement shows how successful a weapon is experience! And we have to remember that until the 1950's, a pastor was expected to be an absolute monarch and that many pastors, even today, have had little encouragement to relate to women as equal partners and close friends. For them, too, the only psychological world they know is threatened.

If we are going to tackle this problem *together*—the only way we *can* tackle it if we want to be Church—then clearly we need to put our feelings "on the table," try to show some empathy for each other, and quietly—though urgently—sort out the other important facts:

NEW TESTAMENT

1. The key fact, obviously, is the message of Scripture. Here we have to be fair to everyone "round the table," for it is only recently that Scripture scholarship has been able to discern that message.

Part of that message is that what used to be thought of as "feminine" characteristics are central to God as revealed in Old and New Testaments. In the Old Testament God revealed "himself" to Moses as "a God merciful and gracious, slow to anger, and abounding in steadfast love and faithfulness" (Ex 34:6)—the kind of person John's Gospel sees in Jesus, when it alludes to that passage (Jn 1:14). At the center of Jesus' life and message—for example in three of his major parables—is compassion, and Paul's central experience of the God who lived in him and in his communities was of gracious kindness.

Another part of Scripture's message is the basic perception of a Christian that we have already seen in Paul's letters. A Christian is someone who is empowered by the Spirit. There is no other power in the Church than that of the resurrected Jesus. The Spirit's presence is shown in different ways in each person, but no way less powerfully in women.

For a Pharisee, like Paul, this fundamental equality between men and women probably meant a revolution in his thinking. However he not only accepted this equality as an established fact of Christian life but he also stressed its necessity.

To see that this is the case, we can begin by taking his statement that for those who are "baptized into union with Christ . . . there is no difference between Jews and Gentiles, between slaves and free, between men and women" (Gal 3:27-28). Here he is quoting a description he had inherited from other Christians of what happens to every Christian at baptism. The divisiveness that stunts and perverts fallen humanity has no place in communities of Christians. Our job as Christians is to show a true and transformed humanity. If we retain these divisions, we cannot do so.

"Am I really maintaining that someone who could write that "it is a disgraceful thing for a woman to speak in church" (1 Cor 14:35) believed in the equality of women?

Obviously, a fair question. But scholars have recently made it possible for us to see that passage in the context of the whole picture.

First, there's the force of that statement in Galatians—not just Paul, the individual, but a commonly accepted statement of what happens in every Christian baptism.

Then there is the fact that Christian women did exercise major roles in Church leadership. Probably in Jesus' own ministry and certainly in the early years of the Church, missionary work was done by partners, who could be couples. Women like Prisca and Phoebe worked with Paul on an equal basis. Apphia, Nympha and others are named as leaders of house churches: the normal context for the Eucharist and for preaching. Phoebe is named "the president" of the church at Cenchrae (up the road from Corinth)— and of Paul (Rom 16:2). Juna—probably a woman—is an apostle (Rom 16:7).

When we turn to the two passages which may seem to contradict all this (1 Cor 11:2-16; 14:34-36), the one thing that all scholars agree is that women are shown to be exercising the highest gift of leadership—prophecy—in Corinthian worship and that Paul and the Corinthians approved of that. There is no consensus among scholars about what Paul is saying about the women's coiffures and the requirements of silence. But whatever he may be saying about those matters must be less important than the acceptance of women in that major role of leadership. We may like to remember that there was no fixed name for the liturgical leader, and that prophets are known to have regularly fulfilled that function.

It is quite true that in other parts of the New Testament,

women are told to revert to a subordinate role. But notice why 1 Peter, for example, does that. "You wives must submit to your husbands, *so that if any of them do not believe God's word, your conduct will win them over to believe*" (1 Pet 3:1). In the world of Asia Minor that surrounded these small Christian communities, the submission of wives to husbands was widely seen by non-Christians as the stuff that sound marriages, and indeed the country's good order, were made of. Few things would have been more likely to alienate people from Christianity than to find that the effect of women becoming converts to Christianity was to subvert married life as people knew it. These and other New Testament texts, where the equality of women seems to be abandoned, need to be seen against the various situations they're trying to cope with.

The valuation of women we find in Paul and the Gospels did not survive because leadership in the Church was eventually absorbed by male clerics, and especially by the bishop. A richly diverse orchestra became a one-man band. Maybe that was necessary, in those centuries, for the survival of the Church. What is certain is that the policy of the Church today is to revert to sharing.

OUR OWN EXPERIENCE

2. In the light of the experience of Christianity that we find in the New Testament, we need to reflect on our own experience.

We have only recently become aware of the extent of women's contribution to the life of the Church. Among those who lead or participate in adult Bible studies or religious discussion, and those who are active in parish renewal and spiritual growth, at least seventy percent are women. More than half of parish counselors are women. Half the readers and more than half the eucharistic ministers are women. By 1984, five of the ninety three parishes in New Ulm, Minnesota were headed by women, and this is bound to spread to many other dioceses. Many of the major diocesan and national enterprises described in this book have been led, with enormous success, by women. The Notre Dame survey of 1985, from which most of these figures were taken, draws this conclusion: "Probably few of us are fully aware of the extent to which we depend on women to conduct the ministries, programs, and activities of Catholic parishes in the U.S." But women may not be ordained priests or deacons; they are excluded from most of the major decision-making, and a perception of them as second-class citizens is still embedded in liturgy and in a range of Catholic customs. *Yet all the developments we have been following in this book depend on the ability to relate and sympathetically nurture.*

In the light of this kind of data, many Catholics are reconsidering the role of women in the Church. Once again, there is increasingly strong leadership from bishops and leaders in other countries.

"There must be a concerted effort by the whole Church to be open to the changing role of women, which has many implications for the life of the Church," the bishops of England and Wales submitted to the Holy See in 1985. Four years before, the American bishops declared that "we see the need for an increased role for women in the ministries of the Church to the extent possible."[3] In 1979 a task force of the Catholic Biblical Association of America gave the view generally held by scholars on "the extent possible" if the New Testament experience is to be accepted: "There is evidence that many of the functions which later were associated with the priestly ministry were in fact exercised by women, and no evidence that women were excluded from any of them."[4]

There seem to be really two questions before the Church about the role of women:

1. Will the matter be allowed to drift, or lapse into a welter of repetitive and sterile argument, or will there be "a concerted effort by the whole Church to be open to the changing role of women"?
2. What about the gifts of the women in the Catholic Church? How grave is our responsibility for giving scope to those gifts? What are our responsibilities to the women themselves, to the life of the Church, and to its service and its message to the world? And if brotherhood and sisterhood lie at the heart of Christian community, are we adequately responding to their pain?

I suggest that there is yet another question. If at first sight it seems extreme, I hope that on reflection it will be judged as reasonable.

Impatience, certainly, is damaging, but should we remain imprisoned in this question for too long? The Church is free, because its one strength is Jesus' Spirit and its one law is love. Its business is to proclaim the possibilities of creative freedom.

Is this really consistent with being grudging, defensive or niggardly with regard to the role of women? Should we not, before very long, say a resounding "yes" to the Spirit so richly evident in many women and then alongside them, with this problem behind us, focus our attention and efforts on the real problems that face us?

Frank Sheed, that modest but major pioneer of lay theology, is said to have been asked by a friend if he would accept being made a cardinal. "Oh yes," he said, with a glint in his eye, "provided Cardinal Maisie Ward [his wife] were sitting alongside me."

What was said perhaps half in jest in Frank's day can be put forward in earnest now. If there were missionary couples in the New Testament, why not now? And if—as is said wisely—a parish pastor's ministry might conflict with married life, why should we not at least ask whether "it might be appropriate in some (perhaps many) cases to ordain a couple for joint ministry''?[5] The point being made here is not any particular strategy, but the responsibility we have to give scope to the gifts and generosity of women—and all God's people—freely, creatively, and wisely, though certainly in union with the whole Church and with the Pope.

"For freedom Christ has set us free" (Gal 5:1). Of course we must take account, in our freedom, of the newness in the Church of the insights about women's roles and the grave problems that many have with these insights. Our freedom must be responsible and responsive. But our main responsibility is to offer a message about human life to the world. The archbishop of Baltimore was surely right about how we should set about tackling the discrimination against women: "We need to lead, not react."[6]

Reflection

- What difference should the New Testament experience make to the Church's present attitudes and practices with regard to women?
- How urgent do you think it is for the Church to tackle this question?
- You may like to reflect on two contemporary views: Fr. Kevin Kelly is an experienced English pastor; Fr. Karl Rahner was probably the most outstanding Catholic theologian of our times. What is your reaction to their views in the light of what we have seen in this chapter:

1. Kevin Kelly visited Peru in 1980. These were his reflections after celebrating Mass in a remote village: "How can we say that it is the Eucharist which is at the heart of our faith and our Christian life and yet deny such communities the Eucharist for lack of a priest, when there is a sister (Sister Therese) available who has as much theology and far more spirituality than most of us priests and who is fully accepted in that community and the one in charge of liturgy?" (*Clergy Review*, 1981, p. 63).

2. Karl Rahner is reflecting in 1977 on the Declaration of the Congregation for the Doctrine of the Faith that women cannot be ordained priests. He gives reasons for his belief that it is open to revision and reform, but must be treated with respect. He concludes a detailed argument by saying: ''Too many demands must not be imposed on this patience, for time presses. . . . The discussion must continue. Cautiously, with mutual respect, critical of bad arguments on both sides, critical of irrelevant emotionalism expressly or tacitly influencing both sides, but also with that courage for historical change which is part of the fidelity which the Church owes to its Lord'' (*Theological Investigations*, Volume 20, p. 47).

Notes

Part 2: Now and Then
Chapter 1: Jesus
1. John Dedek, *Chicago Studies*, Fall 1981, p. 300.

Part 3: Today
Chapter 2: The Rediscovery of Community
1. *Called and Gifted.*
2. Thomas Sweetser, *Successful Parishes*, Winston Press, 1983. p. 2.
3. *Origins*, March 13, 1980, p. 623.
4. Thomas Sweetser, *op. cit.*, p. 5.
5. *National Catholic Reporter*, February 1, 1985, p. 14.

Chapter 3: Who Does What?
1. *Called and Gifted.*
2. Dennis Geaney, *Emerging Ministries*, Andrews & McNeel, 1979, pp. vii-viii.
3. *National Catholic Reporter, art. cit.*
4. *Origins*, March 26, 1981, p. 643.
5. Dennis Geaney, *The Prophetic Parish*, Winston Press, 1983, p. 90.
6. *The Report of the Nottingham Diocesan Assembly*, 1984, p. 31.
7. Thomas O'Meara, *The Theology of Ministry*, Paulist Press, 1983, p. 33.

Chapter 4: Sharing Responsibility
1. *The Parish: A People, A Mission, A Structure*, 1981.
2. *Ibid.*

3. *Ibid.*
4. *Called and Gifted.*

Part 4: Tomorrow
Chapter 1: Communities
1. Kevin Kelly, *Clergy Review*, February 1981, pp. 61-63.
2. *National Catholic Reporter*, May 25, 1984, p. 18.
3. From a speech to a conference in Bruges, June 1985.
4. *The Tablet*, May 15, 1982, p. 476.
5. *Origins*, August 4, 1983, p. 166.
6. Catholic University Study on Vocations (director Dean Hoges), *National Catholic Reporter*, December 16, 1983.
7. Michael Hornsby-Smith, *Clergy Review*, July 1983, pp. 243-245.
8. Abbot Thomas Keating, *Origins*, July 2, 1981, p. 106.
9. *Cross-Currents*, 1982, pp. 106-107.

Chapter 2: Becoming ''A Light to All People''
1. William E. Diehl, *Christianity and Real Life*, Fortress Press, 1976, pp. v-vi.
2. Liverpool, 1980, St. Paul Publications, 1981, p. 87.
3. ''Toward a Church with a Worldly Vocation,'' in *Challenge to the Laity* (ed. Russell Barta), Our Sunday Visitor, 1980, p. 87.

Chapter 4: Sharing Responsibility
1. *Origins*, December 28, 1978, p. 443.

Chapter 5: ''Experts in Humanity''
1. *Origins*, May 6, 1982, p. 743.
2. *Origins*, June 11, 1981, p. 51.
3. *Called and Gifted.*
4. *Origins*, December 27, 1979, pp. 450-453. The Pontifical Biblical Commission in Rome agreed overwhelmingly that a prohibition against women priests cannot be supported from the New Testament.
5. Bernard Cooke, *Ministry to Word and Sacrament*, op. cit., p. 654.
6. *Origins*, September 16, 1982, p. 214.